MAKE YOUR FUTURE SELF — PROUD —

Discover New Opportunities, Change Your Fate, and Dominate Your Destiny

SHAQUILLE MOORE

INTRODUCTION

> The best piece of advice someone could ever give you is, *"Do yourself a favor and make your future- self proud."* - **Shaquille Moore**

We are all in our current positions in life because of our past decisions and actions, whether they were accomplishments or mistakes. Most people don't realize that the everyday decisions and choices they make in the present will directly have a great impact on their future.

You may have read *Choose Your Own Adventure* as a child, where you were presented with two options at the bottom of the page. If you chose the wrong option and the character ended up dying, you could always cheat by going back and choosing another alternative. Even in games such as *Grand Theft Auto* and *Call of Duty,* if you're currently playing a mission, and you make the wrong decision at a particular moment, your character will die. You will then have to restart the mission and make a different decision to progress further in the game. Literally, every decision made in the present will affect the future.

There are many fascinating movies that involve time travel, such as *Back to The Future, Terminator, The Butterfly Effect,* and *The Avengers.* A similar theme reoccurs -- someone needs to go back in time and change the past in order to correct a mistake that negatively impacted the future. But they needed to be careful because if they deviate from the mission and change something else in the past accidentally when they get to the present, things could be different or worse. This is because of the Ripple Effect -- a different choice or one significant change can lead to a whole new series of events in the future.

Think about your own life. Imagine you or your guardians enrolled you into a different church, mosque, college, or youth club rather than the one you went to. A lot of the people you met at these functions; you may have never encountered. This would mean that your friendship circle could possibly be completely different. Your childhood memories and experiences would be totally different, and you may have become a more successful person today, or worse, homeless. It would be extremely advantageous if we could go back in time to correct what we individually consider our biggest mistake or prevent an incident from occurring. Although many of us would love this opportunity, unfortunately, time travel is fictional, and you cannot change the past. But there is something you could do now to enhance the future.

What if you could change the present? Wouldn't it be better to make a strategic decision in the present that would benefit your future self? Instead of the characters in these movies wanting to go back in time and change the past, what if they made better decisions, in the beginning, to prevent that mistake or incident from occurring in the first place?

WHAT DO YOU WANT YOUR FUTURE SELF TO LOOK LIKE?

Everybody has goals, whether they are clear or vague such as desiring to be successful. Don't worry if you don't have clear goals yet, this book will teach you how to become successful and achieve any goal you set your mind to.

In 21st Century Western culture, many aspire to become millionaires and billionaires one day, but only a few achieve the desired outcome. The popular narrative is to go to a university and graduate to get a high-paying 9:00-6:00 job, so you could buy your own house and live happily ever after. However, let's say you wanted to become successful but had no desire to go to a university, would it still be possible to become a millionaire or billionaire without attending university? From the late 90s following the deaths of Biggie and Tupac, 9/11, and beyond, there has been a rise in the number of conspiracy theories surrounding government corruption and the

Illuminati. Also, there were a lot of suggestions that every major celebrity was in the Illuminati, and they sold their soul for money and fame. Furthermore, the television studios, record labels, and news broadcasts were all secretly controlled by this secret society, and you could not become accepted on any of these platforms if you were not part of the prestigious organization.

After 2010, perceptions slowly shifted. This was the year *Instagram* was formed. Other platforms, such as *Facebook* and *Twitter,* started to explode in popularity. Then, *Snapchat* and later *Tik Tok* was formed a few years later. Individuals were seen taking advantage of the development of social media and using these platforms to release their own content that would make them go viral. These viral stars and Master of Social Media appeared on national news platforms because of the exposure of their talents and hard work ethics. The perspectives shifted from needing to join the Illuminati to become successful to if you have a talent or good business idea and you take advantage of social media/internet then anyone could organically become successful.

Today, we have the power to achieve anything we want with the assistance of modern technology. There is no excuse not to take advantage of the times. Do yourself a favor and make your future self proud by setting and achieving your goals.

YOU HAVE THE POWER TO SHAPE YOUR OWN DESTINY

Some of us can recall a victory in our past we are proud of having accomplished. We are proud of the decision we made, at that moment, which led to making that accomplishment successful. Your aim now is to live in the present and be aware that your current actions will have a direct effect on your future self. It is wise to be cautious about not taking any action that could deter you from achieving your future goals. Always avoid making decisions that are a threat to your future self. This is an excellent tactic to ensure that you will avoid making decisions that will lead to a negative series of unfortunate events in your life.

There are things that all humans are guilty of at some point in their lifetimes, such as negative thoughts and feelings. The Law of Attraction states that negative thoughts and feelings can attract negative outcomes, but positive thoughts and feelings can attract positive outcomes. James Arthur Ray, a philosopher featured in *The Secret*, a classic book that speaks about the Law of Attraction, stated, "Our current state of affairs, results from our past decisions and actions." This means that who you are today is based upon the decisions and actions of your past self.

If you are self-made rich today, it is because you made excellent decisions in the past to create a business, earn a high income and effectively manage your finances. Jeff Bezos became a billionaire in the 21st Century because of his past decisions and actions in the 90s that led to the creation of Amazon which experiences an ongoing growth in today's marketplace.

From a reversal perspective, you may be in a current situation that you are not proud of because of your poor decisions and actions in the past. Prison inmates are currently serving sentences because of their poor past decisions and actions. People are in debt today because of their past decisions and actions regarding spending confusing needs and wants. Relationships fail because of past decisions and actions of one or both people involved. It is important not to blame yourself for your current situation if you are unhappy with it. Maybe you didn't know any better. You may not have been aware at the time of what was the best decision and action to take. Likewise, you may not have known that your decisions and actions will create your future.

The good news is no matter what your circumstances are today, you can make your future self proud by making excellent decisions and actions from now on. This book will teach you how to improve the way you decide and react to events, so you can focus on the path of claiming victory for your future self and having the power of who you will become in the future.

Make Your Future Self Proud will teach you how to reevaluate your thinking process to make the best decisions and actions in the present. It also contains many historical and modern-day examples in the most entertaining form of the power of decisions and actions so you can learn the secrets to success from others while learning techniques you can also use.

Make Your Future Self Proud is the ultimate guide for how the everyday person can do themselves a favor and become more successful. Only you are responsible for your own success, but this book will show you the basic principles you can follow to create the best possible future version of yourself.

Achieving Financial Goals

Many people want to become millionaires and be financially free, but they don't know how to even make six figures, until now! Financial literacy and education are key for you to achieve your financial goals. This chapter is going to share how entrepreneurs think and behave financially, so you can learn the skillset and mindset that you need to apply in order to achieve your financial goals.

Strategic Thinking

You must be clever when dealing with people. The decisions and actions you take, especially when dealing with people, will have a positive or negative result in the future.

You owe it to yourself to be ten steps ahead of everyone and see how a move will play out before deciding which decisions and actions will be the most beneficial to you.

Opportunities Come to Those Who Create Them

Life is full of opportunities. Many people would be more successful than they are today if they took more opportunities that came their way. A major problem is that not everyone will take risks. By being unwilling to take risks, they will waste the opportunity.

Some of us have a different issue. We can find it difficult to spot and recognize opportunities that are right in front of our eyes. This chapter is going to teach you how to spot opportunities, the importance of taking risks, and how to become a high achiever. Ultimately, it is up to you whether you want to take the next opportunity in front of you or lose the chance.

Reading The Room

We all desire power and for things to benefit us. The ability to understand how people around you think is vital for knowing how to influence them to do the things that you want. By understanding how using emotional intelligence can be applied as a powerful tool, you can interpret people's thoughts much easier and learn how to predict their next moves. By reading the room and knowing in advance what your opponent's next move will be, the power and leverage is in your hands to benefit from.

Avoid the Joker or Become Part of the Circus

Having the wrong people around you has caused others to lose empires, million-dollar businesses, and many other things. By associating yourself with the wrong people, their misfortunate and bad traits can have a dangerous effect on your ventures. The longer they are around, the greater harm they can cause, and you will ultimately be the person suffering the consequences of their actions. In a world filled with winners and losers, heroes, and villains, you must avoid the losers and the villains at all costs, or your story will end up like theirs. Remember, you become like the people you are around.

Reinvent Yourself

You are the master of your appearance and how other people perceive you. You have the power to change things and make improvements that will ultimately create more power and respect for your future self. The person who will accept things and not make improvements is doomed. If you want others to view you better, then this chapter will teach you the cheat code for how anyone can adapt their appearance and change the way others perceive them.

The Power of Silence

The greatest moves are made in silence. Not everybody needs to know your next move until you want to reveal it. At times, when we are not silent, we can also reveal too much which can create liabilities. Your silence instead will make you appear more mysterious to others, and it will be harder for people to discover things about you that you don't want them to know. Do not allow emotions to distract you from your goals, remain calculated and silent if you want to accomplish great things.

Master the Art of Influence

The elite and most powerful people understand the importance of having control and influence over the market to achieve their goals. It is always preferable for you to understand how to use influence and persuasion to further your own agendas in social and business relationships.

Learning how to influence doesn't mean that you need to be manipulative, instead, this chapter will teach you how to impact the behaviors, choices, and opinions of others to accomplish a result that's mutually beneficial for both of you.

How to Dominate Your Future

If you want to accomplish greater things in life, then you need to have greater goals. When you commit to a greater goal and decide to proactively act on it, you will perform inevitably greater which will yield greater results. This chapter will teach you how to eliminate distractions, focus on mastering your craft, and outperform others within your field so that you can create the best future version of yourself.

If you want to start working on your future, start now.

This book has a lot of powerful knowledge to share, with a lot of gems and nuggets within each chapter. I wrote it so that it is entertaining and an easy read for people who rarely read books. The intention behind this book is to educate you and influence you to make better decisions today so that you can create a better future version of yourself that you are proud of. For many people, this may be the first book they would have read from start to finish. I highly recommend that you take notes on the things that resonate with you the most. Share the principles with your friends if you believe they could learn something that you've read in this book.

CHAPTER 1

HOW TO MAKE YOUR FUTURE SELF RICH

> *Formal education will make you a living; self-education will make you a fortune.* - **Jim Rohn**

Out of all the billions of people living across the world, many people want to know the secret of how to become rich. Many people work hard every week, but their pay doesn't reflect their efforts. There are lots of people who work jobs they don't really enjoy just to pay their bills. They dream of becoming rich in financial security and the ability to spend money on things they enjoy and be able to help others.

The richest people in the world have more money than 99% of the rest of the population, with entrepreneurs such as Jeff Bezos, Elon Musk, Bill Gates, and Mark Zuckerberg surpassing over $100 billion each within the last few years. These people didn't become successful because they got lucky, **they became successful because of the effect of their thinking and behavior**.

Your thinking has a direct result on your behavior and actions, which will lead to a following series of events. Many people won't become millionaires or reach the same level of success as the world's richest people because they do not have the mindset to attain and retain wealth. The thoughts and behavior of a wealthy person are totally different from the average person, which is why a wealthy person receives greater financial results. If you are interested in changing your life financially and learning the mindset of a wealthy person, then guess what; we are going to get straight to the point you are about to find out right now in this first chapter how to make your future self, rich.

The secret to being rich is you need to become **Financially Literate.**

Financial Literacy: How money works, how someone manages, invests and expends.

WHY DO YOU NEED TO BECOME FINANCIALLY LITERATE?

It's not about how much money you make, it's about how much you can keep! MC Hammer was a famous rapper and dancer in the 1980s who released the smash hit *U Can't Touch This* and created a net worth of over $30 million. However, despite the wealth, he ended up filing for bankruptcy and lost a lot of his money because he kept spending too much on personal luxuries and his staff. Have you heard other stories about previous lottery winners or celebrities that became multi-millionaires, but a few months or years later they spent all their money and became broke? Or people who are part of a rich family or have been in a relationship with a rich person, when they stop receiving money, they end up going broke? These people all have a similar thing in common. They could earn more money than most people would ever earn in their lifetime, but they were not financially literate, so they ended up blowing all their money. It is important to realize that you can win the lottery or have a high income, **but if you are not financially literate, you will never be rich.**

THE DIFFERENCES BETWEEN RICH AND POOR PEOPLE

1. **Rich People buy assets, and poor people buy liabilities they think are assets.**

In the classic personal finance book, *Rich Dad Poor Dad*, Robert Kiyosaki relayed that rich people buy assets and poor people acquire liabilities they believe are assets.

Asset: Something a person or company owns that generates money.

Liabilities: Something that takes money out of your pocket.

Liabilities are harmful because these are usually consumer goods and nice things people purchase but they don't need. The result is liabilities will unnecessarily take more money out of your pocket.

Rich people have an unconventional relationship with money. Instead of spending their income on personal luxuries, they invest their money into assets that will generate more income for them. Don't be fooled by all the celebrities you see buying flashy cars, jewelry, and nice things. You may think that the average millionaire spends thousands whenever they want and always purchases liabilities, but this is the wrong assumption to conclude. You have not viewed their financial statements, and some of them make enough money from assets that they can afford to budget a portion of their income toward luxury items to maintain their lifestyle.

2. **Rich people understand the value of money, poor people are reckless.**

Many of us have come across shows on television such as *Shark Tank* or *Dragons Den*, where an entrepreneur seeks investment for their business and the investors believe they have a good product, but the investor thinks the entrepreneur has asked for too high of a valuation. This happened when Jamie Siminoff appeared on the show *Shark Tank* and pitched *Doorbot*, the first video doorbell made for smart phones, He asked for a $700k investment for a 10% stake in the company. The investors didn't believe the product was worth a $7million valuation, so he left the show without a deal. A few years later, he rebranded his product, changed the name to Ring, and raised investments from Richard Branson, Shaquille O'Neal, and a few other investors. In 2018, Jamie ended up selling Ring to Amazon for over $1 billion.

Understand: The investors on *Shark Tank* who Jamie originally pitched to, didn't think the product was a bad idea and not worth an investment. Also, they could all afford to invest his initial asking price of $700k if they really liked the product. The problem was they didn't believe the product was worth $700k for only 10%. They believed Jamie had over-valuated the company, therefore making the idea of investing $700k into his company, not an attractive offer. Just because some of the investors are billionaires, it doesn't mean that they are going to spend $700k on a business investment opportunity just because they can afford it. Rich people are not concerned about whether they can afford to spend money on a product or service, they are more concerned with whether it is worth the money they are about to spend. If the Sharks believed that *Doorbot* was worth $700k for 10%, they would have been willing to invest. Rich people understand the value of money and are willing to invest if they believe it is a good investment. They will not invest just because they can afford to. Poor people will always keep spending money if they believe that they can afford it.

3. **Rich people understand long-term investments, poor people think that anything that sounds like a good investment probably is.**

The Florida Rapper, Rick Ross, who became an investor in multiple *Wing Stop* franchises, received a positive reaction on social media when he announced he was providing his son his very own *Wing Stop* franchise for his 16th birthday present. This type of thinking shows the mindset of a rich person. Poor people will put money into their child's savings account, which will lose value because of inflation, but a rich person will purchase stocks and bonds for their children, so their equity increases over time. It is important to understand the basic concept if you want to be rich; you want to work on investing money into assets that pay you – let your money earn you money.

4. **Rich people look for new opportunities. Poor people hate taking risks.**

Surprisingly, the majority of rich and poor people come across similar headlines in the media and investment tips. For example, many people have heard about investing in Bitcoin before it took off at the beginning of 2021, but many didn't want to invest because they saw it as risky. Rich and poor people have completely different mindsets. When it comes to money, poor people generally don't like a challenge and they are not willing to invest money into new things to make money.

5. **Poor people need money to stay afloat, rich people need money to build their future.**

Poor people want money so they can cover their bills. After they paid their bills, they spend the additional money they have on non-essential items. Instead of saving and investing, which may take a while to reap the benefits, they would rather spend money on entertainment and gambling. If you have traveled around the U.K., you would have noticed that there are more fast-food shops and gambling shops in the poorer areas. This is because gambling is legal throughout the U.K., and poor people are more likely to use gambling shops with the intention to instantly win money so they can put food on the table and afford to purchase more luxury items.

6. **Rich people desire to master their craft by working after hours and investing in self-education. Poor people are not interested in working for free or seeking an advanced education after their traditional schooling.**

> *"Formal education will make you a living; self-education will make you a fortune."* — **Jim Rohn**

In 1985, Steve Jobs, the founder of *Apple* resigned from *Apple.* After he and the newly appointed CEO had different perspectives on the future of the company. After Steve was fired from Apple, he then developed a new company called *Next Computer* and funded *Pixar*, which was originally known as the *Graphic Group,* which was part of the *Lucasfilm* computer division. In 1995, *Pixar* and *Disney* partnered together, and Steve Jobs executive produced the box office success *Toy Story*.

However, things at *Apple* were not going so well. After Steve left *Apple,* he launched the *Power Macintosh*, the original version of today's Mac Computer which was losing the company a lot of money and *Apple* was almost close to bankruptcy. In order to save the company, *Apple* decided they needed Steve Jobs back, so they purchased *Next* in 1997 for $429 million and 1.5 million shares of *Apple* stock.

Life is about putting in the work after hours to master your craft. Steve Jobs told his biographer he used to work from 7:00 a.m. to 9:00 p.m. every day when he was running *Apple* and *Pixar* at the same time. This hard work paid off. One product created by *Next* called *WebObjects* was used with *Apple's Macintosh* hardware to develop the *macOS* and then later adapted to *iOS*. His other company, *Pixar* produced more movies such as *Finding Nemo* and *The*

Incredibles, and then was purchased by *Disney* for $7.4 billion.

Rich people are happy to invest in themselves by working after hours to master their craft, read books to change their mindset, or attend courses and seminars to learn new skills or gain new qualifications that can be used for new work opportunities. They are willing to spend now because they understand they will earn more money long-term with the benefits of the new course. A poor person is not willing to invest in themselves or spend any additional spare time or money on education for self-improvement. They focus on working to afford their bills and use their free time on entertainment and socializing with family and friends.

MASTERING THE POWER OF SELF-DISCIPLINE

> *"The very first step to building wealth is to spend less than you make."* — **Brian Koslow**

Let's recap on how to become rich. We have learned at the beginning of this chapter that to become rich, you need to be financially literate.

Why do you need to become financially literate?

It's not about how much money you make, it's about how much you keep. Okay, so how do I become financially literate then? **You need to master the power of self-discipline.**

The first step to mastering the power of self-discipline is becoming frugal, so you are economical and strict with your spending habits. Instead of paying for an expensive meal on your lunch break at work, buy a cheaper alternative. Most people struggle to have any real chance of ever becoming rich because they spend money as soon as they get it. As you have learned above, a rich person is conservative with their spending habits and looks for the best value when spending money. Understand this -- every time you spend money, money comes out of your bank account, and it will keep decreasing. These transactions add up quickly, and the less money you spend every month, the more you will save and use to invest in assets. By mastering the power of self-discipline, when you get income from your job or any source, you will pay yourself first and not waste income on unnecessary things.

In the book *The Richest Man in Babylon,* it introduces the concept of paying yourself first. To provide further clarity, this means that when you receive monthly income, you should set aside money for bills and necessary expenses, and the rest should be dedicated and placed into your savings account. It is also important to not confuse luxury expenditures with necessary expenses.

PAYING YOURSELF FIRST

YOUR PERSONAL PROFIT and LOSS FORECAST

Main Income Source	
Income Source 2	
Income Source 3	
GROSS PROFIT	

EXPENSES

Rent / Mortgage	
Traveling Expenses	
Utility Bills (Gas, Water and Electricity)	
Telephone	
Food	
Subscriptions (Netflix, Spotify ETC)	
Telephone	
Travelling and Motor Expenses	
Entertainment Budget	
Other	
TOTAL EXPENSES	
Net Profit (Gross Profit - Total Expenses)	

You will need to create a separate bank account to save money. To pay yourself first, you need to know all your personal monthly expenses, so you know how much net profit to send to your savings account, after receiving your monthly income. As you have budgeted all your monthly expenses, including your entertainment costs, you can transfer the money left over in your account to your savings accounts. If you continue to do this every month, your savings will increase.

Barbara Cochran, a multi-millionaire real estate investor from New York City who appears on the ABC show *Shark Tank*, appeared on *The Ellen DeGeneres Show*. When answering fan-related questions, she stated it is wise to have a set monthly budget called 'mad money.' If you earn $1000 a month and live with family, you should budget $200 a month toward things that you like to spend on. If you look at the example Profit and Loss statement, you will see there is an expense related to entertainment. It is very important to have a fixed monthly budget to spend on entertainment such as restaurants, bars, activities, or whatever you like to do for fun. Think of it as expenses to cover hobbies or having fun. You should aim to keep it very minimal and only up to 10% of your monthly income if possible. As you know the more you spend on entertaining yourself and having fun, the less you will be able to put away for savings which can be used to invest in assets to become rich. Remember the ultimate decision to pay yourself first is down to you, as it's your future!

If you own your business, in most jurisdictions, business owners have the greatest tax advantages when they operate as a company or a corporation. Many expenses that would have come out of their personal accounts, such as travel, phone bills, restaurants, hotels, and more, can be used as a tax-deductible business expense against their annual company profits. If your personal expenses are reduced, you can benefit by saving more of your monthly income. Reach out to a professional tax advisor, accountant, or bookkeeper if you would like specific tax advice based on your individual circumstances.

"Try to save something while your salary is small; it's impossible to save after you begin to earn more." — **Jack Benny**

The decisions you make whenever you receive your monthly payments will have major effects on your future. If you want to be rich, then you need to learn how to keep the money you earn, and the only way to do this is to have strong self-discipline and be frugal. Be realistic and frugal with your expenses, don't worry if your profit isn't very high. This will mean that you will need a secondary source of income. We will discuss this later in this chapter.

Most people will never be rich because they do not do their future selves any favors by spending the majority of their paychecks every month. You can enjoy life being frugal. It's not about starving yourself. You just need to reduce your expenses and don't buy things at a premium price.

Frugal Tips

- Cut down on takeaways and eating out.
- Use cashback websites and voucher codes.
- Purchase makeup at wholesale prices.
- Take advantage of purchasing a new phone on finance and use a sim-only contract.
- Shop at discount stores, and always look for a discount when buying items.
- Get a tax-free savings account.
- Use *Sky Scanner* or other comparison websites to book holidays. Also try to avoid traveling in July and August as prices are much more expensive for the same destination as opposed to June, which is usually cheaper.
- Amazon damaged goods – look for the lowest price.
- Use loyalty cards whenever possible!
- Don't purchase over one pair of trainers within 3 months.
- Purchase good quality clothes as they last longer than those of a cheaper quality.

FEAR AND GREED

Many business and financial markets, including the stock market, are motivated by fear and greed. People fear not having money, so they do their best to find a job or invest what they can into a get-rich-quick scheme to eliminate the fear of missing an opportunity to earn money.

Greed makes people think of the things they can buy with that money, which leads to them wanting more. Generally, being greedy is bad, instead, it is better to have a strong desire to make money. You need to have a good reason to motivate you to be rich. The reason must be strong enough that it will keep you disciplined and train you to make smart financial decisions, as well as remain frugal. Over the next few days, think of a reason you want to be rich. Without this reason, it may be hard to remain frugal and maintain the important skills of financial literacy.

WHAT WILL YOUR SOURCE OF INCOME BE?

You must start from somewhere, therefore desire is critically important. If you have a powerful reason as to why you want to be rich, this will motivate your brain to think outside the box and take advantage of opportunities that come your way.

I mentioned earlier in this chapter that poor people work for money and look for jobs so they can buy nice things. However, it is important to note that there is nothing wrong with getting a job to build your savings. Your initial source of income can be anything you want it to be if it is not illegal (we will discuss the disadvantages of illegal income later in this book). The goal is to make as much money as you can initially so you can have savings. Savings are very important because they will give you the power to make smart investments and buy assets when the time is right. As you know, rich people buy assets so their money can work for them, but you need income so you can save money to afford to purchase an asset.

Set a goal to earn a higher income and become a master within your field. There are so many various career options or industries for you to work in. Research how much the top earners within your prospective industry earn every month and year. If you must attend courses, seminars, or read books by people who are already successful within the industry to further your research, then do whatever you have to do. Then, evaluate whether you can replicate or be inspired to do what they do. If you are going to learn, learn from the best!

Successful people don't just have one source of income, they have multiple streams. Even the highest-paid athletes have secondary income from advertising, investments, and other ventures. Michael Jordan became the first NBA player to become a billionaire because of his business ventures and endorsements outside of playing basketball. He also worked with Nike to sell his own brand of sneakers called Air Jordan, which has generated over $1 billion in sales for Nike.

You should use your secondary income to cover non-fixed monthly expenditures such as vacations, festival tickets, and other special occasions. It should also be used to cover emergencies that are unexpected and fines. Never, ever dip into your savings account to cover emergencies. Remember, your savings account is for your future only. If you need funds to cover an unexpected cost, having a secondary income will motivate you to work harder in order to cover these expenses. Let's say you work a 9:00 to 5:00 and want extra money to pay for a holiday. Your secondary source of income could be a second job that can be worked in the evening or even on the weekends. Your pay will increase, and you will have more money available to cover expenses and save every month.

THE POWER OF PASSIVE INCOME

Active Income is money earned from trading your time for money, which is typically your principal job. You can also refer to active income as earned income. You're agreeing to complete a task or a service for financial reward within a specific time frame.

When you start earning money, your primary income will be your principal job. Your plan to earn a secondary income shouldn't just be to earn a second job. This is small thinking and unambitious. You want to practice exchanging your money for time, as opposed to exchanging your time for money.

Transform your life by focusing on researching what assets you could purchase or create that will generate a secondary income source for you that's passive. The amazing thing about passive income is that it **requires minimal effort** and when it increases in value, you will earn more money.

Renting out a room, cryptocurrency investments, selling a book, starting a YouTube channel, selling products online, or other ways to earn additional income. This is different from earned income, which is income received from your job, which is paid to you through your salary, hourly wage, or commission. Most people believe that financial freedom only applies to millionaires or billionaires who live luxurious lifestyles. This is not the reality!

Financial freedom is when your **passive income is greater than your monthly expenses.** When you're first starting out, your monthly expenses will most likely be covered by earned income, presumably your job. But over time, you must practice developing the skill of generating enough passive income that it completely covers your monthly expenses. Instead of trading all your time for money through earned income, your money now works for you, and your expenses will be covered every month through passive income generated from your assets and investments.

THE GAME PLAN FOR BUILDING WEALTH

> *You could have a $100million, but if you don't have a game plan, it's going to be gone!* – **Floyd Mayweather**

If you cannot control your spending habits when you have less than 6 figures, how could handle a bigger amount of money? Most people are poor because of their own poor decision-making. They do not know how to discipline themselves to not spend the money that they earn. If you want to build wealth, it is important to have a game plan for how you want to achieve building wealth.

First, you need to have a savings target of how much you can save in a year. You want to analyze your monthly income to project how much could you really save every month. Then times your monthly savings target by 12, and then you will have your projected savings target for the year. If you have any side hustles or any sources of income where you can earn more money within a certain season or period of the year, then increase or decrease your monthly savings target according to each month. You want to ensure that you try as hard as you can to make each monthly savings target accurate and realistic.

Once you get into the habit of having as much income as possible whilst storing it in your savings account. You need to develop savings targets starting initially from £1000, then £10,000, £25,000, £50,000, and £100,000. A good way to achieve these goals is to project your income every month, quarter, and year. Then, at the end of each month, analyze your finances like you are operating as your own company. Did you reach your goal this month? You must know your saving targets. This will motivate you to avoid spending money on things that you don't need so that you are closer to your target.

After you have reached your savings target, you will understand that with self-discipline, you have been able to accomplish one of your first financial goals. For your second year, you still want to project how much you could save this year. With the money you have saved for your first year, you will need to be prepared to take a small proportion out so you can make calculated investments into assets or ventures that potentially produce additional income. Remember, if you want to become wealthy, you must be aware that due to inflation and low-interest rates, all money saved in your bank account will depreciate over time. So always be on the lookout for new assets to invest a small portion of your money. There are various types of assets you can invest into

- **Properties -** which are good because it increases in value over time and produces monthly rental income if you have tenants. You can also buy unmodernized properties below market value, refurbish them, and sell them for a profit.

- **The Stock Market** - is good for investing in the long-term, as the right company can grow over time and your initial investment can grow. For example, if you invested in *Apple* in 2006, you could have purchased the stock for $1. In 2020, the stock price reached $100. You can also consider investing in ETFs and Index Funds which represent a basket of the strongest companies within a country or sector.

- **Digital Assets** - such as Cryptocurrencies and NFTs. The price of Bitcoin, Ethereum, and other Cryptocurrencies has increased over the years. The value of non-fungible tokens (NFTs), which are unique digital items that are stored on the blockchain network, has also increased. Many people's initial investments have increased over time, and some have earned millions through their investments in digital assets.

- **Starting your own business -** is a great idea after doing your own research and if you believe that your idea could make a difference to the market as well as become profitable.

Remember this book is written for educational and entertainment purposes and should not be considered as financial advice. Always research thoroughly, do your own due diligence, and seek financial advice from a regulated financial advisor before you make any investments. All types of investments present their own level of risk to your capital.

FAILING TO REMAIN FINANCIALLY LITERATE

> *"Money is only a tool. It will take you wherever you wish, but it will not replace you as the driver."* — **Ayn Rand**

We have learned to be rich we need to be financially literate, therefore you must master the power and self-discipline and be frugal with your income. We understand that we need income to build our savings, so we can buy assets and invest in opportunities when you're ready. I need to warn you there is no point working hard if you're going to spend all your money in a few months or even worse at the end of the month. If you cannot master the power of self-discipline and remain frugal in order to keep the money you make, then you will never be rich.

Instead, once you build your income, keep it in your savings account and remember this very important rule. **NEVER DIP INTO YOUR SAVINGS UNLESS YOU NEED TO USE THE MONEY FOR AN INVESTMENT THAT YOU BELIEVE HAS BEEN WELL CALCULATED.**

KEY ADVICE TO YOUR FUTURE SELF

This first chapter has taught you to start building wealth, you need to earn money from a job or another source of income that covers your monthly expenses, and then save most of your net income. Self-discipline is such an important skill from an early stage because when you get to the stage in your life when you earn $10,000+ a month, you will have more money available to invest in assets as opposed to spending more on liabilities.

In the long term, it is very important to make money from things that you enjoy and doesn't cause you stress or make you must look over your shoulder.

Think about what you enjoy. What are your hobbies, and interests, or what inspires you? Imagine a career that you think you will excel well in terms of accomplishments and will be good at. Research the salaries to determine whether it pays well and try to figure out a strategy of how to maximize your income within this industry by exploring the opportunity for you to create your own business and compete within the industry, too. As you know, all private sector career opportunities are run by public and private companies. Instead of preparing yourself to work for these companies, always think long-term, and consider whether you would be good at running your own company instead, where you will earn a lot more money. Then look at the options and evaluate what actions you will need to take in order to get there.

CHAPTER 2

STRATEGIC THINKING

Plot and plan like all good generals – ***E.A Bucchianeri***

The human mind is our greatest asset. We all possess a hidden untapped power within ourselves to accomplish great things and achieve anything we set our minds to. Many people today lack self-esteem and believe they can live a greater life than they currently have or accomplish goals that most people would consider too big. It's not totally their fault. If people who are doubtful and scared surrounded you to take risks, you may not know better. From reading this book, you will learn that certain things are possible that the average person could never imagine themselves achieving. What you choose to do with the knowledge you are about to gain is totally up to you.

From a biological perspective, there are two aspects of the human mind -- **the conscious and the subconscious mind.** The conscious part of the mind contains your thoughts, feelings, and awareness of your surroundings, which can influence decisions. This is the part of the mind that most people acknowledge and are aware of. The subconscious part of the mind contains everything that has been gained from the conscious mind and stores your memories, motives, and feelings. It accepts whatever you put in it, including your thoughts, statements, and experiences. It will store even dangerous and harmful things in your subconscious mind because your brain accepts all your conscious thoughts and beliefs into your subconscious. Therefore, you want to be extremely careful with your thoughts and words.

Negative and destructive thoughts consciously will become subconscious habits that will influence you to behave and make decisions that will only attract more negativity. Your subconscious doesn't have the ability to reason as your conscious mind does. When you say, "I don't want to be late," or "I don't want to fail this exam," you are suggesting to your subconscious that you want to be late and fail. It is crucial to make positive suggestions instead, such as "I want to be early," or "I want to get a high score in this exam." This will train your subconscious to accept these things and make your brain function to make this a reality.

The Law of Attraction states that your thoughts create your future life and they become things. You owe it to yourself to consciously think positive thoughts because without your consent they will be stored subconsciously and influence you to behave and act positively. As Tasha Hoggat stated, “Nothing has a greater influence over your life than your thoughts whether they are negative or positive.”

When you think negatively, you are not encouraging yourself to make decisions that will lead to positive outcomes. Most importantly, you are indirectly training your subconscious to accept negative results in your life. An ideal way of getting rid of negative thoughts is to create a new habit of finding a positive solution that you are comfortable with, every time you think of something negative. This type of thinking will help you when you come across a crisis or an unfortunate event. Curtis Jackson also known as the rapper 50 Cent had to declare bankruptcy in 2015 when a U.S federal judge ruled that he owed $5 million to Lastonia Leviston, the ex-girlfriend of rival rapper Rick Ross for posting her sex tape online, and $17.2 million for allegedly stealing a headphone design for his “Sleek by 50 headphones”. When he filed for Chapter 11 bankruptcy, he stated his current net worth was $4.4 million but his debts were estimated at around $32 million. On social media, people were seen making fun of 50 Cent for being broke, but he didn’t allow this to discourage him. Instead he decided to think of an ideal way to find the most positive solution to resolving his bankruptcy case. The following year in 2016, he made a deal with the court to pay $23 million in the next 5 years, and he managed to pay the debt in full the following year.

Interpretation: Are you wondering how did he manage to pay off the debt early? In order to deal with difficult or unpleasant situations, you must believe that you can overcome them. This self-fulfilling prophecy that you can overcome adverse situations requires you to substitute a negative thought with a positive one. In 50 Cent's scenario, he realized that if a judge can make him pay a fine for breaking the law, then he too could make others pay fines to him if he could prove that they broke the law too. He ended up filing a lawsuit for legal malpractice against his former attorneys and was awarded $13.65 million. He was also still earning money at the time for music royalties and his new TV show *Power* which rapidly grew in popularity around this time.

Understand: Positive thinking is associated with positive outcomes. When you focus on finding solutions and assessing the positive outcomes of a situation, you create positive energy which increases your ability to achieve positive results. 50 cent's positive thinking enabled him to resolve his bankruptcy case and grow *Power* to become one of the most successful shows on cable TV.

THE LAW OF CAUSE AND EFFECT

The Law of Cause and Effect states:

> Every **effect** has a specific and predictable **cause.**
>
> Every **cause** or action has a specific and predictable **effect**.

This means that the position we are in today is the effect and the results of a specific cause. Causes are the everyday decision and actions that we make. Every decision, whether big or small, will create a series of events that will have specific and predictable effects on our future. If you want to achieve success in any field, then it will come because of specific causes and actions. This means that the right decisions and actions will eventually lead to success in the field.

The law states that everything happens for a reason, whether good or bad. Therefore, everything that happens results from a specific cause. It is very important to be self-aware of your thoughts, feelings, and actions, and ensure that they are positive because they are causes that will manifest into specific and predictable positive effects. As the *Old Testament* states, "...whatever a man reaps, he sows."

WHAT IS STRATEGIC THINKING?

Most people are generally reckless. They decide in the heat of the moment based on their feelings. They don't consider the results of their actions; they only regret their actions when they must bear the consequences.

If one takes a step back before they made decisions and focused on their long-term objectives, it will be easier to evaluate what would be the best decision to make. The problem many of us have is that it's not natural to always think with strategy and therefore is important to train your mind to think strategically before making decisions and actions. Strategy is defined as planning for success and tactically using moves or methods to achieve a goal. When you think strategically, you are a step closer to gaining an advantage in every situation and event that you experience. You are teaching yourself to calculate the outcomes of your actions before you take them, so in turn, you can assess if you are about to make a good or bad decision.

If you are aiming for success, you must reassess your entire way of thinking and learn the art of strategy.

In many games, the best players always use strategy to defeat their opponents. In Chess, you will win the game by forcing the enemy king into a checkmate. A good player will predict moves during play and will skillfully calculate the probable outcomes before deciding what piece to move. You must be alert and keep track of all your pieces on the board to protect yourself and win your opponent's material. Strategies and tactics shouldn't just be limited to games; they should be used in every scenario in life to maintain power and achieve the results you desire. In a corporate environment, it is essential for businesses to use strategies to determine how to achieve long-term plans for success and be constantly ahead of their rival competitors. If Blockbuster used strategy, it could have been more prepared for the technology threat streaming services such as Netflix used, which wiped out the DVD rental business model forever.

In imperial history around 748 BC, the Assyrian Empire (now modern-day Iraq) had an extremely strong military which gave them the power to dominate the Mesopotamian lands. They had successfully conquered many Syrian, Arabian, and Egyptian territories. King Tiglath Pileser III set an important precedent for all future Assyrian kings. He stated that an Assyrian King must have control over a Babylonian Empire because the local Kingdoms, Elam and Medes, would always be a threat. If Babylon didn't remain neutral, these Kingdoms could join and take up arms against the Assyrians. After many years of battling rivals for power over the Babylonian throne,

King Esarhaddon decided to make his son, Ashur, the new Assyrian King, and his other son, Shamash-shum-ukin, the new Babylonian King. This should have made the Assyrian Empire stronger than ever, but instead, it led to the Empire's downfall. The brothers kept interfering with each other's affairs and Shamash became hostile, which gave birth to The Great Rebellion and caused the military to lose valuable resources fighting a pointless battle. As the military weakened, Nabopolassar, a few years later, assumed the Babylonian throne and was able to defeat the Assyrians in battle. The rival powers seized these opportunities to capture the Assyrian territories and the empire fell forever.

Interpretation: When you need to make decisions, and you know you have something to lose, it is always best to proceed with caution. Ashur became too ambitious and wanted to pursue his own adventures and agendas without considering how it would affect the Assyrian Kingdom or his brother's wishes.

Understand: There are consequences to all actions, especially when you offend the wrong person. You want to practice considering how your rival or the other person will respond to your next moves and what the worst-case scenario may be. Think like you're playing Chess or Checkers. Would your next move make you more vulnerable to an attack by your opponent? What is the best way to reach your endgame without weakening yourself?

It is in your best interest to consider the consequence and the following result of your actions. Everyone, at some point, is guilty of derailing and not making the decisions that are in their best interests. Remaining focused and alert to the dangers of taking the wrong actions are key to your future survival.

Every community, network, and market contains people with various personality traits. People naturally prefer to communicate things from their own perspective and do not always consider how others interpret them. Inevitably, without using consideration for other people's feelings when speaking, many people will naturally clash with each other and have petty conflicts. Back in 2015, Drake released one of the best diss tracks of all time *Back 2 Back*. The beef started because Meek was upset about Drake not promoting his album. Drake had tweeted Future's album *DS2*, a few days earlier, so Meek didn't understand why Drake didn't tweet *Dreams Worth More Than Money*. Instead of considering how to address this issue in the best manner, he decided to expose Drake by tweeting that Drake doesn't write his own raps. He wasn't prepared for Drake's calculated response which led to Drake releasing two diss tracks within four days, *Charged Up* and *Back 2 Back*. Everybody loved *Back 2 Back* and Meek's response to it was viewed as unsatisfactory by the fans. The popular opinion was Meek lost the rap beef.

At one point, shortly after the beef, it looked like Meek's career was over, but Meek was able to recover. So how did Meek recover from this loss and manage to still become a successful artist? Meek realized he had worse conflicts with people in his hood that involved serious violence and shootings. If he could make amends with former enemies in nearly life-and-death situations, then he could resolve his feud with Drake. He started to respond to interview questions at radio stations saying he was open to speaking to Drake and that he believed they could move forward. Eventually, Drake caught wind of this, and both forgave each other and made music together, again.

From a reversal perspective, you will realize that not all disputes are as public as Drake and Meek's beef. Usually, the other party isn't always aware that someone is holding a grudge against them. Over time, you will learn people can hold grudges against you for many years and some of those people will always be a threat to you.

SOLUTIONS

A) When someone holds a grudge against you.

Grudges are so dangerous. Many people have memories like elephants, they will remember everything. Some people are unpredictable, and you never know if and how they may plot against you. Think of it this way. If someone holds a grudge against you this will clarify you as their enemy. Even if you are in a position where making enemies and offending people is inevitable, why would you allow someone to hold a petty grudge against you that is unnecessary? Not everyone is choleric or outspoken enough that they will let you know instantly if they have an issue with you. Remember, you may deal with those who keep their emotions inward and will not offer you the luxury of informing you about their grudge against you very strategically. Do not assume someone is weak because they haven't voiced their opinion. Everyone experiences frustration, but some people will stay quiet because they don't know how to express their frustrations. Remember, you don't know who this quiet person you underestimated will become in the future.

Do you think Ja Rule and Irv Gotti realized how much of a threat 50 Cent could be in the future when they heard he had just been dropped by his label Columbia after being shot nine times? They didn't care that 50 Cent held them responsible through association, and underestimated that he would recover physically, let alone sign a new deal with

Eminem and Dr. Dre becoming one of the biggest artists of his era.

If you prefer a lifestyle with fewer disputes, then it is important to create an environment where people feel comfortable discussing their issues with you. If you suspect someone may hold a grudge against you, it's better to have a conversation with them and address the topic that caused a potential misunderstanding. Observe their tone, choices of words when speaking to them, and their body language. Once a person feels comfortable discussing their issues with you, it will amaze you what you will learn.

B) When you are holding a grudge?

Nobody likes to feel insulted. We take offense when others are rude, disrespectful, or hurt our feelings. Whatever the other person has done to you, whether it's a transgression against you or someone else that you care about; they are now the problem, the enemy, the antagonist! Now, if you are comfortable with confrontation and being aggressive, you will challenge that person head-on. But if you don't like confrontation, you may prefer to secretly plot against them as many other passive aggressors would. Both options are a waste of time if they aren't going to lead to anything productive.

The worst part of holding a grudge is because you are still angry with someone, it doesn't mean that the other person is aware or still thinking about the situation. The harsh reality is most of the time, the person you are angry with doesn't know or care that you are unhappy with them.

Think of all the people who have wronged you in your lifetime. Do they care about how you feel toward them? Do you think they are concerned that you are holding a grudge toward them? Do you think that they are remorseful? Probably not, or they would have attempted to apologize to you. There is no point in being angry with someone who doesn't even care about the situation. Take the loss and move on. Forgiveness is the best solution, do yourself a favor and let grudges go so you can move on.

DO YOURSELF A FAVOR: LEARN FROM OTHER PEOPLE'S MISTAKES

The book *Make Your Future Self Proud* that you are reading now is not a politically correct book. This book addresses genuine issues that happen in society. In society, as you know, many people commit crimes, especially for financial gain. This section is going to focus on people who break the law to make money.

Whether someone steals, sells drugs, or gets involved in any other type of organized crime, for most crimes that are committed today, someone has already gone to prison in the past. Some people who have gone to prison for financial gain have even become famous characters such as Pablo Escobar, El Chapo, and Frank Lucas, which has led to movies and documentaries being made about their stories.

Many people today still make similar mistakes and believe they won't get caught. As Bismarck said, "Fools say that they learn by experience. I prefer to profit by other's experience." It is so advantageous to learn from someone else's mistakes instead of making them yourself.

Nobody is above the law. Pablo Escobar, El Chapo, and Frank Lucas were all clever businessmen. Just because they sold drugs, it doesn't mean that they couldn't have been successful if they were legitimate businessmen. All these major crime figures have a common problem -- they treated their criminal enterprise and activity as a full-time career. They tried to set up systems to grow and expand their business, employ staff, and donated money back to their communities. However, they failed to understand there is no longevity in criminal activity.

Today, people fail to realize you can work hard and put a lot of effort into illegal activity to the point where you can allegedly generate a million dollars in a day like Freeway Rick Ross, but you cannot grow the business forever and pass it on to your children as assets. You also must be careful about who knows what you are doing because the wrong person could inform the police. It's better to quit while you are ahead. Money is power, but it has less power when it appears illegitimate. Law enforcement and government agencies will be motivated to take your hard-earned money and assume it's all illegitimate if they have enough strong evidence against you. It's not worth it!

Learning from other people's mistakes or experiences can apply in various circumstances and business industries. If you're trying to flip houses, you can read reviews and watch blog videos from others who have experienced flipping houses and have made mistakes. By knowing what their mistakes are, they can be a tool guide for making sure you avoid those mistakes too and just focus on achieving your goal.

CHAPTER 3

OPPORTUNITIES COME TO THOSE WHO CREATE THEM

If opportunity doesn't knock, build a door - **Milton Berle**

In 2018, Merck Mercuriadis, Elton John's former manager, co-founded the British investment company Hipgnosis Song Fund with Nile Rodgers. Merck understood that publishing pays in the music businesses as songs earn continuous royalties every time they are played.

Back in 1985, the pop star Michael Jackson had capitalized from owning other artists' publishing by buying ATV Music for $35 million, which held the rights to many of The Beatles' hit songs. Sony Music eventually purchased half of ATV and then the rest in 2016 for $567 million. Paul McCartney and John Lennon, from The

Beatles, have unfortunately lost a reported $715 million worth of earnings from this deal. Merck offered artists large upfront payments for their publishing, so he could earn from the long-term royalties instead of them. Some of his deals included $25 million to Lady Gaga and $100 to Justin Timberlake for his entire music catalog including 100% of all of Justin Timberlake's copyright, ownership, and financial interests as a writer.

Everyone in the music business knows about publishing and royalties, but many will not risk their own money and buy another artist's publishing. Instead, larger companies such as Sony Music, Warner Brothers, and Universal Music acquired publishing from artists. Universal Music bought Lil Wayne's catalog for $100 million and Bob Dylan's 60-year catalog of 600 songs for $225 million.

Merck was clever; he spotted an opportunity, understood it, and took a calculated risk by buying the publishing upfront. His portfolio is now worth over $1 billion. Merck is a shark in the tank. You too can create opportunities for yourself and achieve high success.

SHARK IN THE TANK

Definition: Someone with a strong desire to succeed who spots opportunities that others don't see and seizes them to achieve results. However, to seize these opportunities, they are willing to take risks.

Real-life sharks in the ocean know to eat, they must seize their prey and be careful not to allow their prey to slip away. As humans, who desire financial success, we cannot let excellent opportunities swipe past us. We need to take opportunities quickly before they expire.

We are going to break down the three principles of how to be a shark in the tank:

1. How to spot an opportunity.
2. The importance of taking risks.
3. Becoming a high achiever.

STEP 1: HOW TO SPOT AN OPPORTUNITY

"Don't wait for the right opportunity: create it." - **George Bernard Shaw**

Many people wait for someone else to provide them with a business opportunity or any chance to earn some extra money. Many people, if left to their own resources, will just apply for a job. You don't want to be the type of person who relies on others, instead, you want to be self-reliant and develop your skills for spotting opportunities that could benefit your future self.

Many entrepreneurs who have taken opportunities and been successful understand the opportunity before they invest in it. If your desire to make money is strong when you come across things that you are passionate about, ideas may get sparked, and you may spot an opportunity.

Curtis Jackson, also known as 50 Cent, spotted an opportunity with Vitamin Water and secured one of the most lucrative business deals ever in Hip Hop. 50 Cent spent a lot of his time drinking water, especially when working out every day. He noticed in many stores the most expensive water brands sold for a lot more than the water brands with no name. This engaged his interest and he decided that he would invest in a water company. One day while at the gym, he came across Vitamin Water; he then set his mind on making his investment. He got Glaceau, the company that owned Vitamin Water attention by drinking Vitamin Water during the filming of another promotional advertisement. Coincidentally, 50 Cent's manager found out that Glaceau was working on a new drink called Formula 50. They offered 50 Cent money to advertise Formula 50 after a meeting was set up, but 50 Cent expressed his interest and passion for selling water and asked them for equity in Glaceau instead. They agreed and even changed the flavor to Grape based upon 50's suggestion. This led to an aggressive promo campaign led by 50 which eventually led to Coca-Cola buying Glaceau for $4.1 billion.

You must have a strong desire to make money and spot excellent opportunities just like 50 Cent did. When you came across something that's within your interests and hobbies criteria, your strong desire to make money can spark an opportunity. Remember, everyone spots opportunities differently. It doesn't have to be an obvious opportunity that anyone could notice. The opportunity simply must be one that sparks your interest, just like Vitamin Water sparked 50 Cent's interest in investing in a water company. If it's something others don't see, that doesn't matter.

Many of the biggest companies in the world began by someone who spotted an opportunity that others didn't see. Ken Kutaragi, an executive who worked for Sony, came up with the idea to create a game console called the PlayStation which was also a multi-purpose entertainment unit that was compatible with playing audio CDs. This made PlayStation the first-ever game console to sell over 100 million units.

The most important principle is that you can see and understand when an opportunity is right in front of you and how you can execute it. When spotting opportunities, always make sure the opportunity is worth your while and there is enough demand for your new endeavor to make it worth chasing.

DO IT BETTER

Another way to spot opportunities is if you see someone doing something and you realize you can do it better. Microsoft saw that Sony's PlayStation 2 found a good niche by releasing a game console that could play DVDs and CDs as well as releasing popular game titles that adults and children can enjoy. So, Microsoft released its own console called the Xbox, which was the first gaming console with a hard drive installed. They also released their own game exclusive, such as Halo and Gears of War.

Google wasn't always the biggest search engine. It initially started off as a research project by Larry Page and Sergey Brin while they were Ph.D. students at Stanford University. Before Google, Yahoo and Alta dominated the search engine market Vista. Google built a better product with comprehensive results and stronger algorithms.

Facebook wasn't always the biggest social networking platform. The social networking market was previously dominated by *My Space* and *Friends Reunited*. Mark Zuckerberg figured out how to offer a better product to suit customers' needs.

FOCUS IS KEY

In business studies, you may have heard of the term niche market, when an entrepreneur focuses on a specific product/service to suit a certain demographic of customers within a larger market. Some people think targeting a niche market doesn't seem fun because of the limitations of the market. But that's the problem. Some people fail to realize that there are great opportunities to be successful by targeting a specific market, as opposed to trying to target everyone.

In 2007, Brian Chesky and his friend Joe Gebba moved into a San Francisco, California apartment and met a software engineer called Nathan Bkechangk. Together, the three offered their apartment as a place to stay for people attending a design conference hosted in San Francisco. Excited about their new business venture, they decided to name it Air Bed and Breakfast, and use their apartment to test if the business would work by providing short-term stays with customers sleeping on Air Beds. After a few successful short-term stays, Michael Siebel from Y Combinator, a Silicon Valley accelerator program for startups, decided to invest in the business. He liked the fact Brian, Joe, and Nathan were initial users of their product, not just as travelers but also as hosts. Being initial users of the product was important to Michael because when challenges occurred, this gave the team the opportunity put themselves in the customer's shoes and imagine what they would have done in this situation. Air

BnB was successful by focusing on its niche; people who needed short-term stays. They understood the product from the consumer's point of view, which helped them ensure that their product made customers happy.

Focus is everything, even an I.T. Recruitment firm focuses on candidates who are looking for jobs within the I.T. industry. It's better to be the biggest fish in the smallest pond than a small fish in the ocean. In other words, it's easier to dominate your niche and do well if you understand the market and customer base.

Fortunately, the world is constantly changing and evolving. There are always new trends and new platforms being introduced. Declines in pure album CD sales and the increasing popularity of streaming music gave birth to Spotify, Apple Music, and Tidal. YouTube created opportunities for video podcasts, content creation, and video radio interview platforms. Instagram created the opportunity for many businesses that attract most of their customers and sell many of their products through Instagram. If you want to be a shark in the tank and spot new opportunities, always look for new trends and changes in your environment. This is the birth of new opportunities.

IF YOU DON'T CREATE OPPORTUNITIES FOR YOURSELF, YOU WILL ALWAYS BE AT THE MERCY OF OTHERS

A final point on spotting opportunities -- if you really want something in life, you cannot wait for the opportunity to be provided for you. You must create this opportunity for yourself.

Years ago, before *Jaws* and *The Color Purple* were made, Steven Spielberg always dreamed of becoming a movie director, but he had no idea how to make this a reality. Who would trust him to direct a big movie without previous experience? Steven decided to go on a Universal Studios tour with a suitcase. He used this opportunity to now befriend other directors and writers, which led to him connecting with Sid Sheinberg who was the head of the production for the television studio arm. Steven showed Sid an amateur film that impressed him enough to get Steven a contract with the studio. Steven Spielberg's first film, *The Sugarland Express,* wasn't a box office success, but he used the lessons and experiences learned to make better movies. He also managed to convince the producers, Richard Zanuck, and David Brown, to allow him to direct the movie *Jaws*, which became a huge commercial success.

Steven Spielberg created the opportunity to get a contract with Universal Studios by finessing his way into the building and befriending the right directors. Without this, he could have been cold-calling all the film studios for years and been ignored. Instead of waiting for the opportunity to be provided to him, he presented his amateur film directly to Sid. You can also learn from Spielberg's story. Be proactive and actively take the opportunities you want, don't wait and hope someone will provide them for you.

In the early 2000s, Kanye West was known as a producer and he made beats for many artists, including Jay-Z. This gave him access to the Rocafella Records office, the label that Jay-Z co-owned with Dame Dash and Kareem Burke. Everyone at Rocafella saw Kanye as a producer, but Kanye didn't want to be known as a producer; he wanted to be known as a rapper. He believed he was as talented as all the other rappers around during that era and wanted to compete with all the other mainstream rappers. After months of trying to convince everyone to give him a shot, Dame Dash eventually signed him to Rocafella. Part of the reason was to avoid losing Kanye as a producer.

After signing with Rocafella, things didn't immediately start progressing straight away. The label still viewed him as a producer and focused on other artists instead. There was another issue too, Rocafella was not willing to allocate a recording budget to Kanye West. Without a recording budget, how would Kanye afford studio time to record his album? He knew that if he couldn't release an album, he would never become the artist that he dreamed of becoming. Kanye West decided to create an opportunity for himself to record his album. He asked others, such as Jamie Fox and Ludacris, if he could record some of his songs during their paid studio sessions instead of Kanye's. He also spent time in the studio while Jay-Z was recording his album *The Blueprint 2*. He freestyled for Jay-Z, and Jay-Z was so impressed he decided to feature Kanye on the song *The Bounce*. This was a major cosign for Kanye. Kanye continued to self-record his debut album *The College Dropout*, and once he was done, all he needed was for Rocafella to agree to a release date.

It looked like Rocafella wasn't taking him seriously as an artist, even after his album was recorded. A year after being signed, there were still no updates on when Rocafella would release his album. However, he was determined to make sure we heard his music. Legally, he couldn't release the album without Rocafella's permission, so he released mixtapes so more people could hear his music in the streets. He had to reluctantly keep producing tracks for other rappers just so he could still afford studio time and record his music video for *Through the Wire*. He had previously released *Through the Wire* on his *Get Well Soon* mixtape in 2002, but he was determined to record a video for *Through the Wire*. A video would be the perfect opportunity for him to convince Rocafella that this single would become a success and create more anticipation for his album. In late 2003, *Through the Wire* ended up debuting 15th on the Billboard 100 charts, which finally convinced Dame Dash to set a February 2004 release date for Kanye's debut album *The College Dropout*. When *The College Dropout* finally was released, it debuted at number two on the Billboard charts, and Kanye's career, as a rapper, had officially begun.

Understand: If you believe in yourself and you want the opportunity to become successful, you must create opportunities whenever you can. If Kanye didn't keep being persistent in convincing Dame Dash that he was more than a producer, then he would have remained a producer. Also, if he didn't release mixtapes, even after being signed to Rocafella, his album may not have been released. Not all artists who sign to a label are able to release an album. Like Kanye, if you believe in yourself and you are willing to create opportunities for yourself, then you too can be successful.

STEP 2: THE IMPORTANCE OF TAKING RISKS

> *"You can measure opportunity with the same yardstick that measures the risk involved. They go together."* – **Earl Nightingale**

The American rapper Ice Cube was originally part of the rap group NWA, and the movie *Straight Outta Compton* was based on his story. After starring in a few movies, such as the 1991 classic *Boyz N The Hood*, Ice Cube decided he wanted to make his own movie. He wanted to make a "hood classic" that showed the fun aspect of living in the hood, so he wrote the screenplay with his friend DJ Pooh. After developing the character Smokey, who was based on DJ Pooh's small period of drug dealing, and Craig based on Ice Cube's cousin, they wanted a movie studio to finance the movie. They were aware they were both inexperienced in writing movies and it would be much harder for them to secure a deal with one of the top movie studios. After seeing how successful the Black American comedy film *House Party* was in 1990, they were interested in approaching the studio that produced and distributed the film, New Line Cinema.

They set their sights on New Line Cinema and after meeting with New Line Cinema, they agreed to produce the movie and approved Ice Cube's choice of director, F. Gary Gray, who had never directed a movie before. However, DJ Pooh could no longer play Smokey, and they required a more experienced actor to play Smokey instead. After receiving the green light from New Line Cinema, they filmed the movie within 20 days on a $3.5 million budget and grossed almost $30 million at the box office. The movie is one of the most memorable Black American comedy movies of all time and is still considered a hood classic decades later.

Although Ice Cube has a successful career as a rapper as well as producing comedy movies, it wasn't easy for Ice Cube to initially produce *Friday*. First, Ice Cube was known as a gangster rapper. He hadn't starred in a comedy before, so he wasn't sure how the movie would be received by his audience. He had never written a script for a movie before, and he had to learn the structure of writing a script as he went along. After spending two months writing the script, he also didn't know if any studio would be willing to produce or distribute the movie. If New Line Cinema didn't want to distribute the movie, then Ice Cube and DJ Pooh would have had to consider financing the movie themselves. There was also a risk of the studio deciding to make alterations to the movie that may have clashed with Ice Cube's original vision. If Ice Cube wasn't willing to take risks, he would have continued his rap career, acted in other people's movies, and never produced his own movie. His Cube Vision Production company that produced some of his most popular movies *Ride Along with Kevin Hart*, *Barbershop*, and *Are We There Yet*; may never have existed. If you are not willing to come out of your shell and take risks by trying new things, you will always risk future success.

FORGOT ABOUT DRE

The movie *Straight Outta Compton* was also directed by F. Gary Gray and produced by Ice Cube. Another person who the movie was based upon and helped produce was Dr. Dre, who was part of the NWA rap group. Toward the end of the movie, Dr. Dre left the label Death Row, which he had created with Suge Knight, and started his own label Aftermath in 1996. Death Row was successful and was well known for the albums by artists such as 2Pac, Snoop Dogg, and Dr. Dre himself. However, Dr. Dre didn't know how well his new label Aftermath would be received. He released a compilation album on the label which was not well received at all, and critics questioned him. Things didn't look good for Dr. Dre until he met Eminem, a rapper from Detroit, who initially caught the attention of Jimmy Iovine, the owner of Aftermath's parent label Interscope. Eminem had just come second in a Rap Olympics competition, but he passed a copy of his album *Slim Shady* Ep to Dean Geistlinger, an intern at Interscope, who shared it with Jimmy. Jimmy was impressed with *Slim Shady* Ep and recommended him to Dr. Dre, who then signed Eminem to Aftermath and released Slim

Shady on his label. Eminem was well-received, and his second album released under Aftermath, *The Marshall Manthers* LP sold over $1.78 million in its first week. Decades later, *The Marshall Manthers* LP is still the fastest-selling album of all time. His friendship with Eminem developed over the years and after Eminem discovered 50 Cent, they both completed a joint venture deal to sign 50 Cent to Aftermath, Shady Records, and Interscope Records. 50 Cent's first album *Get Rich or Die Tryin* sold 872,000 copies within his first week and his second album *The Massacre* sold over $1 million copies within the first week. Both albums were executively produced by Dr. Dre.

After the success of his label Aftermath, Dr. Dre took another risk by entering the headphone business with Jimmy Iovine. Many headphone product ideas introduced by other companies had failed in the past and there was no guarantee that his new venture, Beats by Dre, would become successful. They decided to launch an incredible marketing strategy by placing their headphones in many major music videos. They partnered with Monster Cable to help them with manufacturing and then HTC decided to purchase a 50% share for $309 million. After focusing on developing good quality products and being constantly innovative, Beats by Dre caught the attention of Apple in 2014, who purchased the entire company for $3.2 billion.

Dr. Dre is successful today because after leaving Death Row, he managed to develop his skill of working closely with artists to produce great records. He wasn't afraid of going into other ventures outside of rapping/producing music, which has earned him most of his wealth.

If you want to be successful in life you cannot afford to not take risks. As Nicola Yoon, the author of the book *Everything*, stated, "Everything is a risk. Not doing anything is a risk. It's up to you."

STEP 3: BECOMING A HIGH ACHIEVER

> *"Achievers don't submit to instant gratification; they invest in the long-term payoff."* - **Darren Hardy**

A high achiever is someone who achieves greater accomplishments than the average person. This could be buying a home or having a 6-figure net worth before the age of 25. If you play sports, this could be winning a major sports competition such as Usain Bolt. You could even be a working professional and end up reaching a top position in your company quicker than the average person due to great results.

HOW DO YOU MAKE GREATER ACCOMPLISHMENTS THAN THE AVERAGE PERSON?

You need to be driven by having goals you would like to achieve, and you must also aim high. Think of your heroes who you will consider as high achievers, whether they are famous or non-famous. They could be in any type of industry, entertainment, sports, or business-related field. No matter what industry, they all must compete against others either directly or indirectly, at some point.

Even if they are not competing against someone, they will always be compared to another person or business in their field to determine who has the greatest accomplishments. For example, the producers of *Avengers End Game* (2019) and *Spider-Man: No Way Home* are competing against every other superhero movie for the highest box office sales. They are not just competing against superhero movies by the rival comic book brand DC, they are also competing against previous Marvel movies. As I am writing this, *Avengers End Game* is currently the 2nd highest-grossing movie of all time, exceeding $2 billion in gross sales. *Spider-Man: No Way Home* was the highest-grossing movie of 2021 and exceeded $1 billion in gross sales within the first month.

As a high achiever, competition doesn't need to be the driving force behind your goals, but you need to be ready to compete against the accomplishments of others. Never be afraid to compete against a great competitor. If someone has done it in the past, you can do it too, or even better.

Why is it important to make high achievements? Making high achievements is important because one achievement can provide the confidence and experience you set yourself on a path to make more achievements. Success breeds success. Your body also releases dopamine, which allows you to feel pleasure every time you achieve something. The more pleasure you receive in the short term from your achievements will motivate you to achieve more in the long term. High achievers continue to make their future selves proud every time they make another accomplishment because they know that **SUCCESS CAN ALWAYS BE REPEATED.**

CAN'T STOP WON'T STOP

The rapper and entrepreneur Sean Combs also known as Diddy has a remarkable story. He started off working as an intern at Uptown Records, where he signed legendary R&B recording artist Mary J Blige. He then founded his own label, Bad Boy Records, and by 1994 he had two successful artists, Notorious B.I.G and Craig Mack. Bad Boy's success continued to grow when he signed more artists to the label such as Lil Kim, Mase, and Faith Evans. By 1996, he signed an incredible 50/50 joint venture with

Clive Davis and Artist Records allowing Bad Boy Records to market their artists to a global marketplace and he retained full control of the label, his artists, and back catalog.

After being successful in the music industry, he became interested in fashion. In 1998, he launched Sean John clothing which has achieved an excess of $100 million in sales in a single year. In 2004, the brand was awarded the Men's Designer of the Year award by The Council of Fashion Designers of America. He didn't just become a lucky music executive who created a successful clothing brand, he created a Sean John fragrance called Unforgettable and he partnered with a company called Diego which launched the Vodka brand Ciroc in a partnership and is now set to be worth over $100 million.

Diddy throughout his career continued to spot opportunities that aligned with his interest and hobbies. Being successful in one venture gave him the confidence to believe he could be successful in others. Diddy isn't a superhuman. A lot of these famous billionaire figures like Bill Gates and Jeff Bezos are humans, just like everyone else. The reason they are high achievers is that they constantly have made decisions in the past that led to future accomplishments. They don't get lucky and make one accomplishment they have a mindset where they are serious about working hard and making movies that lead to big results. Therefore, Floyd Mayweather became one of the highest-paid athletes of his time. The confidence of having a clean record where he had never lost a boxing match, gave him the courage to pitch a new business deal with Showtime. This deal gave him the power to keep 100% of his gate revenue from his fights and sign a 6-fight 3-year deal between 2012 and 2015 after HBO refused to pay him what he believed he was worth.

Upon reflection, think about what you would consider your highest achievement. Remember, the power of association is very important, and you are more influenced by the people around you than you think. If you believe that you're not surrounded by high achievers, then try to expand your circle to positive and influential people that work hard to accomplish their goals.

NEVER SET A GOAL WITHOUT A DEADLINE

If you have goals or ideas you want to accomplish, then you need to set a deadline. In life, we come across many ideas that unfortunately are not executed. This is because life is full of distractions and if you do not fully commit to something, it's harder for you to master your craft.

If you have an idea that you are passionate about and you have decided this is something you want to commit to, then you need to start telling your friends and family who will support your idea and not use it against you, about your idea. The reason why others must know about your goal is that you need people to hold you accountable if you do not reach your goal.

External motivation is important because people can help and support you to keep you encouraged toward achieving your goal. As the author of this book, when I started writing it, I had to tell people that I was writing a book. Why? I had never written a book before, and I knew the concept of this book was going to resonate with millions of people across the world. I knew writing this book would be a good idea and others would approve of it. I also knew that over time, my friends and family would ask me for updates on the progression, which was important to encourage me to finish writing.

CHAPTER 4

READING THE ROOM

> *When dealing with people, remember you are not dealing with creatures of logic, but with creatures of emotion.*- **Dale Carnegie.**

In the 16th century, Niccolò Machiavelli wrote a guide to a prince about how to maintain rule over his subjects within his kingdom. When advising whether it was better for a prince to be feared or loved, being loved depended on a prince's subjects; but being feared depended on the prince. It was up to the specific prince to choose what he believed would work for him as both options had their advantages. It was important that a prince must do what he can to avoid hatred! A prince could only inspire hatred if he interfered with the women or property of his subjects. There were no bank accounts or cash in the 16th Century, so property meant anything owned such as land, gold, animals, or another type of asset.

Why was it necessary for a prince ruling a kingdom to avoid hatred? Machiavelli wanted the prince to understand that if he wasn't on good terms with his people, too many people would conspire to kill the prince for the benefit of the kingdom. Throughout history, many kings and rulers have been assassinated. Those who have sparked less hatred, fewer people will want to conspire against him and the few who would always be a threat would have less support amongst others. Although you are not a king or ruler who has to worry about potential assassination attempts because people within your kingdom have a reason to hate you, it is very important for you to avoid hatred and conspirators today in the 21st Century.

Why would someone hate you? People will only hate or strongly dislike you **if, according to them, they have a justified reason to hold a grudge against you.** The reason could be petty or could be the result of a dispute. However, if someone has a reason to strongly dislike you, they are very likely to do things that will work against you.

Why are modern-day conspirators dangerous? Kings and rulers had to worry about conspirators attempting to assassinate them. Today, you must be cautious of conspirators attempting to assassinate your character. Everyone who holds a grudge against you for whatever reason is a potential conspirator. You also can't control whether one of your enemies will elevate into a new position of power or influence, where their voices become louder. They could easily attack your reputation and harm your ventures. It's also always a bad feeling when a group of people who are associated through friendship, business, or acquaintance has a mutual dislike toward you. When your name comes up in a discussion, the conversation and plots will never be in your best interests. Have you noticed that when someone gets exposed for something negative on social media, other people who have had a negative experience or have a reason to hold a grudge also start speaking up? The further the news spreads, the happier the people who hold a grudge against you become.

You must view everyone who hates or strongly dislikes you as a threat. If they are associated with other people who dislike you, expect them to consider conspiring against you. On the other hand, if the person who hates you doesn't know many of your peers or other potential conspirators, you should never underestimate them.

Social media advances every few years and you never know who will connect with who and compare notes about you. It's wise to try to clear the air with everyone today who may hold a grudge against you. If it's possible to resolve the issue, then resolve it! If you are unable to contact the person, or the person isn't interested, then at least you have tried. Wouldn't you prefer to live in peace with less conflict?

In the present, you also want to avoid wasting time with pointless new conflicts. Be mindful in the present and in the future not to give people reasons to hate you or hold a grudge. Aim to practice this and you will have less to worry about long-term. The secret to resolving disputes, handling complaints, and improving your relationships with people is emotional intelligence. If you want power and to gain advantages in business relationships, then developing your emotional intelligence is vital.

Emotional Intelligence is defined as the capacity to be aware of, control, and express one's emotions, and the ability to handle interpersonal relationships judiciously and empathetically. You are about to learn what the different aspects of emotional intelligence are and how to build your knowledge by breaking it down into three powerful steps.

STEP 1: MASTER YOUR OWN EMOTIONS

When you react, you let others control you. When you respond, you are in control. - **Bohdi Sanders**

During the rise of the Roman Empire in the 1st Century AD, many provinces were controlled by senators. In today's U.S. government, congressmen and senators vote for and against new laws passed through congress. Senators during the Roman Empire had a similar role, they agreed to laws, governed provinces, and sometimes had command over armies.

Agrippina was the fourth wife of Emperor Claudius and the mother of the famous Emperor, Nero. She was always consumed with wanting power and attempting to use her position to rule the Empire as if she was an emperor. The senators always noticed she wanted to rule the Empire through her influence over the emperors and for every senator who challenged her; she made Claudius believe they were a conspirator. Therefore, every senator who she saw as a threat was executed. When Claudius became vulnerable, she killed him by poisoning him and killing his son, Britannicus, from a previous marriage. Once her son Nero became Emperor shortly after Claudius' death, Agrippina's ambition to control the Empire grew even more. Nero was an inexperienced emperor. He raised taxes which created a lot of hostility, and he eventually lost the respect of many, leading to rebellion across the empire. His biggest problem was his mother, Agrippina. She wanted to control everything that he did, including his personal life, and who he chose to marry and have sexual relations with. After Nero realized, that Agrippina was attempting to control him through his wife, Nero got frustrated and left his wife for his new mistress. As Agrippina was fond of Nero's wife and she didn't want him to be with his new mistress who she didn't have influence over, she desperately tried to interfere with his new relationship and do everything in her power to end it. This backfired. Nero became so frustrated he had his wife and Agrippina executed.

Interpretation: We all need to remember what our long-term goals are. Most roman sources credit Agrippina as a very ambitious person, but they were critical of her intentions. There was nothing wrong with her wanting a bit of power and security by marrying an emperor and having her son become the potential heir. But what exactly was Agrippina's long-term goal? If her long-term goal included maintaining power, then she went about it in a bad way. She exercised poor emotional intelligence when she let her position get to her head by wanting to control everything her son did. If she had mastered her emotions and was more self-aware of how her interference in his personal life would affect her son, she would have realized that her actions were always going to frustrate her son, which ultimately led to him resenting her and then having her executed. Whatever her long-term goal was, it surely didn't include dying the way she did.

Understand: The harsh truth is that if you fail to master your emotions by managing your personality and certain behaviors, it could prevent you from achieving your long-term goal. When you are tempted to think or act within your emotions, you must always remember what your goals are. Always ask yourself, if I act impulsively because of my emotions, would this have a positive or negative effect on my long-term goal? If negative, then you may want to reconsider your actions.

When you stay focused on your long-term goals, you will become more cautious about not committing actions that could deter you from achieving those goals.

Therefore, power is not for everyone! Most people, at some point in their lives, elevate into a good position in their career or within their community where they can earn better money or even have more power and influence than they previously had. However, because they don't know how to master their own emotions, they eventually end up doing something that weakens them, and they end up fumbling the bag. If you want your future self to remain in a good position and continue to positively progress, then being calculated and having control over your emotions is essential, or you can never maintain power forever.

We all have unique character traits and personalities. Some of us are more sensitive to other people's words and get easily offended by what someone might say to us, while others are more affected by other people's actions. Everyone handles anger differently. Some may keep their frustration bottled up within them and when it explodes, it can be physically or verbally destructive. Others have no issue addressing people who have upset them and immediately deal with a situation that has upset them.

Understand: It is important to be self-aware of your own emotions and what things will upset or offend you. Then you must practice how to express your feelings to others without hostility and aggression, which usually aggravates a situation. People can resent you based upon something you said in a burst of frustration and not everybody forgives. You want to do yourself a favor by committing to addressing things that have upset you head-on if you want to improve your relationship with the person or the morale of your current environment which you share with your aggressor. You need to understand your emotions and be more aware of what things upset you, so you can forecast the best way to cope if a similar situation arises.

NEVER REACT IMMEDIATELY WITHOUT STRATEGICALLY THINKING

In 44 BC, Julius Caesar was stabbed 23 times to death by conspirators from the senate who accused him of being a dictator and wanting to rule the Roman Empire as a king instead of an emperor. Mark Anthony, a loyal supporter, and friend of Julius Caesar arranged the funeral and wanted to rule the empire with the support of everyone. He gave away a lot of Caesar's treasures to form alliances while allowing some of Julius Caesar's conspirators to control other provinces. The following year in 43 BC, a political alliance known as the Second Triumvirate was formed between Mark Anthony and Lepidus, who used to work for Julius Caesar, and Octavian, who was Julius Caesar's adopted son. This agreement meant that no wars could be waged without the approval of the Senate. Not long after, Mark Anthony and Octavian accused Lepidus of being disloyal. They exiled him to rule Africa and shared the rest of the Roman Empire between themselves.

During this era, it was common for people to marry to maintain power and alliances, so Mark Anthony married Octavia who was Octavian's sister. Their alliance took a dramatic challenge when Mark Anthony decided a few years later to marry a beautiful and irresistible woman from Egypt -- Cleopatra. What made matters worse was Cleopatra had a son called Caesarion who was also Julius Caesar's son from their private affair. After marrying Cleopatra, Mark Anthony eventually dismissed his former wife Octavia which made Octavian even angrier and gave him further justification to strongly dislike Mark Anthony. Octavian knew at this point he had to destroy Mark Anthony, but he had to master his own emotions by deciding to only make a calculated decision to plan his next move, instead of doing something impulsive. He also had two problems.

First, Mark Anthony still had a lot of power and support within the empire, and he couldn't exactly spark a civil war within Rome, especially when he still had a political alliance with him. Second, Mark Anthony was married to Cleopatra who had a son with Julius Caesar prior to this marriage. Cleopatra and Julius Caesar's son Caesarion was technically an heir to the Roman Empire meaning that he was a major threat. Octavian had to avoid making a wrong and impulsive move otherwise he could risk being killed himself.

Octavian realized that he needed to declare war against Mark Anthony with the support of the Senate, but it couldn't appear as a civil war, so he decided to strategically make his personal rival appear to be an enemy of the entire Roman Republic. He also knew he would have to transfer the power of his army over to the senate to appear as if he was a loyal supporter of the Republic, unlike Mark Anthony. At the same time, he didn't want to lose power over the army just to please the senate. So, he made the most skillful move possible. He realized he could secretly maintain power over the army behind the scenes by secretly controlling the senate, who would now control the army. He also got rid of individual senators who he saw as a threat, then created his own rules and criteria for how people can join the senate. With this new level of power and influence over the senate, he waged war against Mark Anthony and Cleopatra, which he eventually won. Mark Anthony ended up dying in Cleopatra's arms, Cleopatra was captured and later committed suicide and finally, Octavian killed Caesarion to eliminate him from being an heir to the Empire.

Interpretation: When emotions are suppressed, it is easier to think of the most calculated move that will favor you and give you power over your rival; it was this type of thinking that led to Octavian changing his name to Augustus Caesar and he became one of the most powerful rulers in history, including the first Roman Emperor. Like Augustus Caesar, you can also accomplish a lot when you suppress your emotions. If you are angered or offended about something, you must have self-control and learn to not immediately react to situations or even overreact to things. When you are distressed, you must practice the skill of holding back and allow yourself time to reassess the situation. If you respond too quickly when influenced by emotions, you can make the problem escalate further and contribute to creating a crisis. You want to create a self-analysis of your emotions. Analyze how you react in certain situations that distress you. Do you make decisions based on your emotions within that moment, or are you more of a rational thinker?

Understand: Not everything requires an immediate response or action, instead, it is better to give yourself additional time to think and examine what the best course of action is. If you're unsure what to do, consider taking advice from someone you trust and respect. Also, never call out someone via your social media for everyone to see including the person you're speaking about. When you master and have control over your emotions, you realize you don't need to express yourself so publicly for attention and sympathy, and you will act less impulsively. Share your concerns about distressful situations with a trusted person in private. The whole world as you know it, doesn't need to know via social media that you are upset. Always be calculated before you respond to things.

STEP 2: HOW TO UNDERSTAND AND PREDICT SOMEONE'S NEXT MOVES

You can only understand people if you feel them in yourself. - **John Steinbeck**

Empathy is a skillful art that is practiced over time and a major component in all human interactions and interpersonal relationships. The more your empathetic skills develop, the easier it is to understand others. Most people take things at face value and believe what someone tells them unless the person has given them a reason to doubt or mistrust them. If you want to understand people's true feelings, you must use empathy and pay attention to more than just their words.

Empathy is observing people's body language, paying closer attention to other people's choice of words, tonality, and facial expressions to understand their emotions, which indicates how they truly feel. After practicing observing these signals over time, you will start to notice cues that will make it easier to interpret human signals. These types of observations are important in relationships whether social or romantic, managing people, sales, parenting, and other fields within your life that you may not initially realize.

Developing the skills of empathy comes from understanding your own emotions and then recognizing them in others. You need to desire and make effort to be empathetic and more conscious of other people's feelings and emotions. You want to be selfless and practice listening more to others and seeing things from the other person's point of view. Think about how they would interpret an experience in their mind, how would it make them feel, and then later respond. Understand that everyone has their own ideas and values, therefore, you may come across people who think completely differently than you. By being sensitive to other people's feelings and how they could impact their future decisions, you will find it easier to see the future moves someone will make.

On a basic level, if you're playing games such as four in a row, Chess, or Checkers, you will understand if you make a certain play, your opponent will respond with a particular move. It is also not always in your best interest to be seen as a threat unless it's your desire to be feared because this can result in people becoming disloyal to you and making moves that may potentially harm you. The Roman Emperor, Caligula, eventually killed everyone he saw as a threat to becoming an heir to the Empire including all his male relatives. He only left his relative Claudius alive because he was physically handicapped and never believed that it would have been possible for him to become Emperor. He was wrong. After Caligula died, Claudius became the 4th Roman Emperor.

You constantly want to be attentive toward observing people's non-verbal cues such as facial expressions, gestures, and body language across various situations to have a greater understanding of how they feel. It is important to notice changes in behavior, even the slightest change, as it could indicate a change in their mood or feelings. Analyze how they behave when they are engaging while they are communicating with you or others. Are they looking away sometimes? Are they folding their arms? You cannot miss these key signals; they are vital in terms of learning how to influence people and understanding what they truly desire. Learn how to register these actions with an emotion or a hidden thought that they have not shared with you.

ANALYZE SITUATIONS CAREFULLY

Earlier in this chapter, I mentioned that hatred led to conspirators; therefore, it is important to be aware of this and avoid hatred at all costs. When you are in a tough situation where conflict may occur, it is important to think about how the other person would respond to your actions. How will your next move, influence their next move? What could it possibly lead to later down the line? You want to use all the information that you have available to you, so you can truly know who you are dealing with. It is vital to consider how strong the person you are dealing with really is, so you can strategically decide if it's best to stand your ground and disagree or if is it better to retreat and offer a compromise. As Sun Tzu said, "Know your enemy and yourself, and you shall win a hundred battles without loss."

If you choose to stand your ground, the decision may not necessarily lead to hatred. It may not be that serious, but it is important to analyze how the way you respond to a situation will affect your relationship with the person moving forward.

Let's say you are a sales manager and the current sales your team earns every month are very crucial for the company's growth. Now imagine one of the members of your team who you manage, has been the top seller for the last 6 months in a row, and he is asking for a pay raise after 6 months of consistency. If his request is fair and at the industry standard, but you chose to decline his request, he could resent you and the company, which could lead to him looking for a new job elsewhere. How would you feel if he started working for one of your competitors instead, and using the skills he developed at your company to enhance your competitor's sales and company growth? Imagine the impact on your company with the loss of his sales and now the new rising competition. Wouldn't it have been easier to give him a fair pay raise that was acceptable under industry standards? Do yourself a favor and always think about how the way you may respond to a situation will affect your relationship with someone going forward.

STEP 3: NEVER OFFEND THE WRONG PERSON

"The only way to change someone's mind is to connect with them from the heart."- **Rasheed Ogunlaru.**

Being more conscious of your own emotions and reading the signals other people's emotions reveal, puts you at an advantage. You are more aware of how human emotions can affect the way situations play out. If someone's emotions will lead to a decision that you may consider a threat, you can now use your emotional intelligence IQ to assess the best way to handle the situation. You could either resolve the conflict with the person head-on or you could empathetically consider the person's next move and prepare a defense.

Kings Charles I became the King of England in 1625 and married a Roman Catholic called Henrietta Maria during a time when England was a Protestant society. He had increasing tensions with the English Parliament over time and after trying to impose certain practices on the Church of Scotland, this led to the start of a civil war known as the Bishop Wars in 1639. Eventually, after losing a lot of men in the battle of Naseby, he handed himself over to the Scottish Army who delivered him to the English Parliament 9 months later in exchange for payment. The English Parliament then put Charles on trial to justify the execution of the King. Charles was eventually beheaded in 1649.

Understand: You must be on high alert and conscious of how your actions can offend others. This will enable you to ensure that you are always attempting to be on good terms with others, if possible. Charles initiated conflict with Scotland by trying to govern the Church of Scotland insisting there should be one uniformed church. This offended the Scots and they violently opposed him. If Charles I made a better attempt to be on good terms with Scotland and Parliament, the likelihood of an open rebellion against him would have been much lower. When you don't consider the other person's next move, it is possible to get carried away by doing things that only favor you fearlessly. This is dangerous because you are less observant of rising tensions and are less considerate of how others may respond to your actions.

As previously mentioned, sometimes we are unaware of the power of enemies. When people hate or strongly dislike you, it can lead to conspiracies or plots against you. The good news is that being aware of these puts you in a powerful position. You can avoid making enemies and prevent disputes from escalating or even happening. It is vital to be aware of how your actions can make a situation better or worse. Remember the principle -- prevention is better than cure. It's better to prevent conflict from even happening as opposed to trying to smooth things after.

At times, you may not even realize that you can offend the wrong person who could even be a close friend or business partner. Suge Knight was a businessman and founded Death Row Records with Dr. Dre in 1992. They released Dr, Dre's classic *The Chronic* album under their label, and then they signed Snoop Dogg and 2pac shortly after. While Death Row was successfully selling albums, Suge Knight was involved in a lot of controversy including a public beef called "East Coast vs West Coast War" when he insulted Puff Daddy at the 1995 Source Awards. Suge Knight ran Death Row like a gangster and used violence, intimidation, and bullying tactics. Eventually, this caused tension between him and Dr. Dre which led to Dr. Dre voluntarily leaving a label that which he owned 50% of shares. After Dr. Dre left, Death Row couldn't maintain its momentum after the death of 2Pac, and Suge Knight landed himself facing myriad legal issues. Snoop Dogg also ended up leaving the label. Dr. Dre then created a new label called Aftermath and discovered Eminem and eventually signed 50 Cent.

If Suge Knight didn't offend Dr. Dre with all his bad practices, the likelihood of Dr. Dre leaving the label would have been lower and Death Row may have still been successful years after the death of 2pac.

The problem with offending people is that you don't always know how they will respond and how their response could harshly backfire. It is important to understand how easy it is to offend someone. First, many people have different things that they may feel sensitive about, and some people can be very sensitive. You won't always know this especially if you are not very familiar with the person. When dealing with a sensitive person, when you discover that may become "too sensitive," you must immediately become cautious of the criticism and statements you make regarding certain topics or issues. If it conflicts with something they are passionate or sensitive about, it will more than likely cause friction between you and that person.

From a reversal perspective, you may be the person who has become offended because someone has made a comment regarding something that you are passionate about. Never overreact because someone has said something that has triggered you. You need to always consider their intent before you respond. Some people may just be insensitive toward the topic and may not have any intention to be disrespectful. If this is a person that you do not have ulterior motives with and you need to play it cool, limit conflict as much as possible to achieve your agenda. Then, the best course of action to take is immediately to address the person who has offended you unless you need time to cool down.

Once conflict has occurred and there is a discourse between you and the other person, it is important to know when you decide to use empathy to understand the experience from their point of view, your attitude and tone of voice will naturally change, which will encourage you and the other person to work toward coming to a solution. Avoid going back and forth about how they initially reacted to the situation, which may have also caused you to become offended. You want to keep the focus on them and be mindful of using the best tone of voice and choice of words. **The wrong tone of voice and choice of words can escalate the situation and make it worse.** Always show respect to the other person. Be compassionate and empathetic with the other person. This will influence you to have the correct tone of voice and words which will help you become steps closer to rectifying the situation.

It is also important to be a good listener. Listening is a key skill for developing emotional intelligence. Good listeners are more sensitive to how others feel, and it becomes easier to the other person's perspective. When you're having a dispute with someone, always aim to find out what actions you display that offended them. This information is vital because it can help you identify any faults in your behavior that you can decide to change and will help you have better relationships in the future. You're not just listening to them for their benefit, you're listening because they can say something that could be way more beneficial to you in the long term.

CHAPTER 5

AVOID THE JOKER OR BECOME PART OF THE CIRCUS

> *"It's rare for a toxic person to change their behavior. More often, the only thing that varies is their target and the blame they place. Because some toxic people are difficult to identify, keep in mind that a victim mindset is sometimes a red flag. So, listen when someone talks about their life and circumstances. If the list of people, they blame is long... it's probably only a matter of time before you're on that list."* – **Steve Maraboli**

The book *Make Your Future Self Proud* covers a variety of topics, but the fundamental principle remains the same. Do yourself a favor by making strategic and good decisions in the present to *Make Your Future Self Proud.* Why is making good decisions important? What are we trying to prevent from happening to us?

Well, most people would prefer to not experience betrayal, misfortune, or disappointment. Although some of these setbacks are unfortunately inevitable, we can limit the risks of this from happening by being selective about who we choose to associate with.

Jim Rohn, a motivational speaker, stated, “We are the average of the five people we spend the most time with.” You’re naturally always going to want to fit in. People often want to belong to a specific group, and this motivates us to participate in certain social and sports activities to strengthen our relationships and build new friendships. Being part of a group is how people survive. The groups we decide to be a part of are so important. The people you speak to the most will influence the focus of many of your conversations. Within your conversations, you will naturally become influenced by the attitude and behavior of the people you spend a lot of time speaking to.

People are more influential and have more power over you than you would think. The right people can have a great impact on your life and make you even stronger. The wrong people can infect your life in a toxic and harmful manner. If you’re hanging out with people who make bad decisions, they will encourage you to make bad decisions too. We are always influenced by the people around us, including how to dress, what TV shows to watch, and which festivals and parties to attend. If what your friends do doesn't conflict with your moral compass, they will probably influence you to make similar decisions to them. Therefore, if you surround yourself with a group of bad decision-makers and unsuccessful people, then the chance of you becoming influenced to also make bad decisions is quite high and you may also remain unsuccessful like your companions. Therefore, you need to carefully guard your mind against what you allow to influence you. Only surround yourself with people that you can learn from and eventually grow into a better version of yourself.

DON'T LET ANYONE HAVE POWER OVER YOU

Some people experience greater misfortunate than others. The wrong people can cause serious misfortune and there is no limit to how fatal it can be. In the *Old Testament*, Samson was a Nazirite given superhuman strength by God. God said to him that if he was to ever cut his long hair, he would lose his strength; so, he kept the secret of his strength a secret. Samson, however, met a woman called Delilah, who had been approached by the Philistines and were Samson's enemies. They had been losing battles with Samson for years and they wanted to bribe Delilah into finding out a way to defeat Samson. Delilah used to repeatedly ask Samson the secret of his strength. He would tease her by saying if he was tied up with fresh bowstrings, he would lose his strength. She would then tie him up during his sleep and he would snap the strings when he woke up. Samson eventually told Delilah the secret to his strength, and she cut off his hair when he was sleeping so that the Philistines could successfully capture him.

Interpretation: Samson ended up being captured by the Philistines who ended up blinding him. If Samson didn't reveal his secret to Delilah, it is unlikely that the Philistines would have ever been able to capture him. Delilah was an infector. An infector is a person who can cause harm to another person or their ventures. Infectors gain more power, the more we associate with them, the more important their role or position is in our life. Samson empowered Delilah by giving her vital information about the secret of his strength. This put her in a position where she could have the ability to cause him harm. Don't give people the power or ability to cause misfortune.

Understand: It's not practical or enjoyable to be cautious all the time. But there are steps you can take in order to protect yourself from misfortune. Your first step should be to always become aware and conscious of the level of harm people can have on you. Once you are aware of this, you can choose how to set limits and boundaries with this person. For example, it could be as simple as not having your partner's contract on a tenancy agreement, so if you have a dispute with them, you do not risk losing your house. If the property is solely in your name, your partner has no leverage over your home.

Limit the effect someone could have on you, your family, or possessions by:

- Concealing information that can be used against you, and
- Learn to become a good judge of character; people will make moves at your expense and won't care how it affects you.

Samson should have learned to become a good judge of character. If he was, he may have sensed her true intentions when Delilah tied him up with his strings during the times that he teased her about the secret of his strength. However, becoming a good judge of character is a skill that must be practiced over time.

WORK WITH THOSE WHO SHARE YOUR VISION

You may decide to work on a project within a business or you simply may want to achieve a goal. If you decide to include others, you need to make sure you are choosing to work with the right people. The right people are those who share a similar vision and foresight as you for whatever you are all mutually working toward. They must believe in the idea and foresee what needs to be done to make it a success.

Curtis Jackson, also known as the rapper 50 Cent, was shot nine times just before Columbia Records was about to release his album. After hearing about the news of the shooting, they decided to drop him from the label. He was still determined to become a successful rapper, so he decided to launch his mixtape campaign in New York City, which started to catch a buzz. His buzz grew so much that it eventually caught Eminem's attention. Eminem had recently launched his album *The Marshal Manthers* LP which sold over 22 million records. He believed in 50 Cent's vision and felt that 50 Cent would be a great artist for his label. Eminem then signed 50 Cent to his label, which gave him access to the legendary producer Dr. Dre who also believed in 50 Cent's vision. Then 50 Cent released his album *Get Rich or Die Tryin* through Shady/Aftermath Records, Eminem, and Dr. Dre's labels and sold over 700,000 units within the first week.

Most people won't share your vision. You must always be prepared to do as much as you can yourself to gain initial momentum. Eventually, when you're at the point when you need to include others for specific purposes, you must be willing to add or remove those who aren't beneficial to your success.

Some people believe that working with the right person means someone with a lot of experience or high status. They're waiting to get hired by the top company in the industry, work with the most experienced management team, or get signed to one of the biggest music labels as a rapper. What many people don't realize is the right person could be among your friends and peer circle, who may not have a high status but has the same vision and foresight as you. Jay-Z is one of the biggest rappers of all time. Believe it or not, no record labels during the 90s wanted to sign him. He recorded his debut album *Reasonable Doubt* and knew it was going to become a major success. However, none of the labels were interested and they all passed. Instead of giving up because none of the labels shared his visions, he decided to create his own label called Rocafella Records with associates Dame Dash and Kareem Burkes. They then partnered up with Def Jam for their distribution network. He was able to sign new artists such as Kanye West, Rihanna, and J-Cole years later after his own commercial success.

Ambition is priceless. Not everyone will see the vision, and you won't always get approval from top executives within your chosen industry. Don't let that deter you. Learn how to use your friends who share the same vision and are willing to work as hard as you. U.K. rapper Stormzy realized this at an early stage and trusted his smartest friend to manage him. He knew his friend didn't have any experience in the music industry, but he knew his friend believed in him and was willing to work hard and learn. He also met his DJ through another one of his friends, which was vital for him to deliver live performances to a high standard from 300-capacity London nightclubs to headlining the Glastonbury and Wireless Festival. In life, you must always bet on yourself, begin your journey and you will come across the right people along the way.

It's been mentioned above that projects are more successful when the people involved have a similar vision and foresight. Passion is the key. If people have a genuine passion for their specific craft, directing, performing, producing, etc., and if you present your idea and they want to work with you, they will always be beneficial if the person is truly 100% committed. This is because when people are truly passionate about something, they will put in as much time as needed to ensure that the project is a success. Think of your favorite movie or the last good movie you watched. Now, there is no way that the movie would've been a success without a few elements.

First, the person with the original idea for the movie would need to pitch the movie to a distributor such as Universal Studios or 20th Century Fox. If the studio likes the idea and believes it can work, then a few producers will be recruited to start the production of the movie. The movie needs to have great actors, so casting will now begin. Each actor will read the script to decide if they like the story and if they believe they can play the character by auditioning well. Even if your father is producing a movie such as Ice Cube producing *Straight Outta Compton*, Oshea Jr. still had to audition to play the character Ice Cube in the movie. In the movie *Coming 2 America* produced by Eddie Murphy, his daughter Bella Murphy still had to audition for a role. After an actor's audition, both the team of producers and executives at Universal Studios would need to approve the actors. The producers also need to choose someone who they believe will be the best director for the movie and the studio will need to approve the director. The director needs to have a passion for directing and love working with actors in order to get the best out of them. Even the stuntmen involved in the movie will need to share the same vision as the director for the action scenes to look good. The costume designers will need to understand the vision in order to make sure the actors are wearing the best costumes. Literally, everyone involved can't solely join the project just for money, they need to have a passion for what they do to ensure the movie gets the best box office numbers possible. They want to make sure everyone sees and enjoys the movie.

Why is it so important everyone involved believes in the project? Every project has a greater chance of success when everybody involved is fully committed to it. Even artists like Drake and Nicki Minaj were rapping and releasing projects before they met Lil Wayne. Drake initially met Lil Wayne through a mutual friend called Jas Prince. After listening to some of Drake's music, Lil Wayne wanted to work with him and introduced him to Birdman. In 2009, they signed Drake to the label Young Money/Cash Money because they believed in him. They were willing to make sure enough money was invested into marketing Drake in order to ensure that he would be a success.

DON'T GET INFECTED

Make Way for The Bad Guy

In the 1983 classic American crime drama *Scarface*, starring Al Pacino, who played the character Tony Montana, was a notorious drug dealer. He claimed to love his family and his friends, but it came with the condition that he approved of their lifestyle and relationship choices. There was a scene in the movie when he went on a rant at a dinner party and said, "Come on. Make way for the bad guy. There's a bad guy comin' through! Better get outta his way!"

Tony Montana was truly a bad guy with traits and intentions. There are many bad people among us who are destructive and unstable. They have a negative impact on others who surround them. Some of your friends can also be destructive and unstable. You could have a good relationship with certain friends and may not initially feel that they may have bad intentions towards you. Things can change over time and once you're on the person's bad side, you will see a completely different side to them.

The solution is to keep as far distance as possible from bad guys. If they are among you at work, school, or any environment where you can't choose who else is there, always try to limit your encounters with them and only communicate with them when it is completely necessary. You may decide that it is better to relocate to work in a more positive and productive environment. It may be wise to enroll your child in a private school where the students move on to better prospects than a public school that is ranked lower. You might want to consider moving to a higher-income housing complex, so you can surround yourself with higher earners. The perks of this are that the crime rate is lower, and you live in an environment with more successful people.

Never Work with Jokers

Many people knew Abraham Lincoln as the U.S President who abolished slavery and many viewed him as a great leader. After winning the 1860 U.S Presidential Election, he decided to appoint 3 of the other candidates who lost against him to his cabinet.

Why would he choose to build his cabinet with former rivals who competed against him in the election? Lincoln was playing the long game. During the time of conflict regarding the status of slavery, he understood that he needed to build a strong team to fight against the Confederates in the south, in order to win the American Civil War. Therefore, he decided to surround himself with the strongest people for the benefit of the nation, it didn't matter to him that they were former opponents.

Understand: We are all governed by self-interest and some level of ego. We can sometimes allow our feelings and personal opinions to distract us from making decisions that would not benefit our overall goals. Barack Obama read about the history of Lincoln prior to becoming president. He decided that he too was going to have a successful government by appointing the best people for the job, despite any personal grudges or previous history. Like Lincoln, Barack Obama also built his cabinet with a team of rivals by appointing Joe Biden as his vice president and Hilary Clinton as his secretary of state, who both had competed with him in the 2008 U.S Presidential Election.

On the other hand. If you decide to work on a project and you can choose who the core members involved are; never work with people who are unprofessional, don't work at a good standard, or are in denial about not having the best skills for that role. They will waste your time, not meet your expectations, and could cause harm.

When hiring and recruiting, play the role of the CEO of a billion-dollar company. You, as this CEO, will only consider hiring the best candidates possible. Right? People are selected based on their skills, and their ability to work well with the other members of their team. When you work on a project, work with the best people available if you want the best results. Avoid poorly skilled and unserious candidates.

Know When to Walk Away

There can be times when your interests may no longer align with your friends, partners, or business associates. Many ignore the obvious that their relationship has run its course. They have a mindset that things will get back to how they were. They let the relationship continue out of loyalty and to avoid confrontation. They know deep down they are no longer happy.

Russel Simmons and Rick Rubin created Def Jam in 1983. Hip Hop albums became a major success and Def Jam was a top label. There was trouble in paradise. Rick started to develop more interest in working with rock and roll artists, while Russel Simmons remained focused on Hip Hop and RnB. Rick decided to leave without any legal battles, and they remained great friends.

When your vision or happiness is on the line, you cannot afford to remain in the situation to please other people. If you don't have to remain in the situation to please other people, or if you don't have your best interest at heart, no one else will. Like Russel Simmons, you must be willing to make tough decisions and walk away.

Sometimes we can be guilty of showing too much compassion and patience for a relationship that needs to end. You may be afraid of confrontation and prefer to be a people pleaser. You may prefer to look for a compromise to not ruffle any feathers. What most people don't realize is that inevitably, you will clash with some people. People have their own unstable issues from their past negative experiences. Some people only do things that suit their own agenda and have no interest in considering compromising or empathizing with others. Their actions may not be malicious toward you, but if it's causing you to clash too strongly, then you need to walk away before the fire gets too hot. It doesn't have to be hostile when you decide to part ways with someone. You can cordially explain how you feel, assess how the other person feels, and then make a mutually beneficial decision. If they want to hold a grudge that's on them, you can't control that. All you can control is constructing the most strategic delivery possible to limit any potential damage.

FINAL PERSPECTIVE

Always be careful who you have around you, and if someone is going to be around you, make sure they are adding value to your life. If you aren't around people who are beneficial to your growth, aim to find the people that you want to be around. Research where they eat food, where they live, and which cities or specific neighborhoods. Where do they go to network with other like-minded individuals? In terms of health and well-being, where do they go to exercise or use the gym? You need to find and surround yourself with people who will add value to your life and not take it away.

Value also must be a two-way streak. You must also bring something to the table and add value to someone's life too, or why would they choose to be around you?

CHAPTER 6

REINVENT YOURSELF

The ordinary people always judge by appearances, and the world consists chiefly of ordinary people. - **The Prince**

STEP 1: BE THE MASTER OF YOUR APPEARANCE

Nothing succeeds like the appearance of success. - **Christopher Lasch**

Human beings are very social and impressionable creatures. They will hold you accountable and form an initial first impression of you based on your appearance. Your appearance isn't just based on the way you look, your clothes, or your hair. It is also your behavior, including everything you say and do that other people can see and hear. If your appearance seems authentic, people will believe you are the person you appear to be. It is essential to be aware of and understand the power of your appearance; you must always be in control and alert to how others perceive you.

In 2016, Donald Trump became the 45th U.S. President. For most of his life, he was known as a rich, successful businessman and a celebrity who appeared on television. Before he became President, he was respected and was an inspiration to many Americans who desired to live the American dream. It wasn't until around the 2016 Presidential election campaign that he made comments which were viewed by many as controversial. The perception of Donald Trump changed from a successful businessman to someone who makes controversial and insensitive comments.

Understand this; the biggest names in the entertainment industry who many consider legends and famous will always lose credibility and respect if they appear to be racist, homophobic, or display some type of sexual predator behavior based upon a newfound discovery that begins to circulate in the news and on social media. It's also very dangerous to be seen as a snitch, whether you are famous or not. The further the news spreads that someone is a snitch, the harder it is for them to recover. You must be alert and guard your reputation against being ruined by saying or doing anything that could damage your reputation.

Most people can think of and recall at least one other famous person whose reputation has gone from being respected to damaged based on various factors mentioned above. Need I mention Will Smith and the Oscar fiasco? As a result, the backlash has been harsh. He was banned for ten years from attending this major event, and his productions were dropped all because of one slap. You must protect your good name and be alert to any decision that could weaken your image. Do yourself a favor, don't spend years building a good reputation, and allow one fatal effort to ruin everything.

You want to keep your appearance clean and avoid bad publicity at all costs. We've all heard the phrase, "There is no such thing as bad publicity." This is false! Not everyone knows how to take advantage of bad situations or find a new opportunity through chaos. Also, there are some things that are extremely difficult to fully recover from; for example, committing a sexual offense. If you have bad publicity for something that is viewed as horrible and cruel to a person who was more vulnerable than you, it will not do your future self any favors.

THE ART OF BEING FEARED

You can inspire fear and respect based on your appearance. A strong man with muscles and 6-foot plus will always inspire more fear and respect than the average man. Why? People naturally will think he has a greater ability to physically discipline them than the average man. On the other hand, a beautiful woman will always inspire fear and respect over the average woman. Why? People will naturally perceive a beautiful woman as higher value and more desirable. The more beautiful she is, the greater the commodity, and she and others will perceive she has greater access to bigger resources.

Your appearance is very important! There are people you may have come across you and others may have feared at one point in life, such as a strict teacher at school or a former boss. It could also be a rival competitor in your industry or someone in your social community circle that is known for defeating people in physical and verbal confrontations.

Machiavelli describes fear by stating, "Fear is bound by the apprehension of punishment which never relaxes its grasp." When people fear you, they assume that you are stronger than you are. They probably have no first-hand experience of having conflict with you, but inspiring fear through reputation will make you win more battles than you ever need to fight. Let's say a new gang member who hasn't established a good or bad reputation yet, decides to start releasing music. Then his YouTube videos feature a few real authentic gang members surrounding him in the video; like Chief Keef's *I Don't Like*. Whether Chief Keef is a real gang member or not is irrelevant. If the music video is so good that it catches the interests of radio stations and normal civilians, people will naturally assume the new artist is about that life. Rival gang members will start to identify this new artist as one of the key members of the gang, based on the music's popularity. That artist will earn even more stripes if a story spreads of them committing a violent crime. Their rivals will take that artist even more seriously. On the other hand, there will always be someone who will target a new artist to gain clout by causing physical harm to them. Also, if a story ever gets out that the artist was injured, robbed, or snitched on someone, that artist may lose credibility in the streets, forever. Reputation is everything!

It is wise to inspire fear, when necessary, as fear encourages respect, and most people will prefer to avoid conflict with you. They will reconsider getting into battles with you, which will always give the feared person the upside. Remember, the presence of a feared person or rumor that a feared person may involve themselves in the situation will always increase the probability of a solution in favor of the feared person. Always be mindful that your reputation precedes you.

USE YOUR IMAGE AS A TOOL TO GET WHAT YOU WANT

Being conscious of your image shouldn't be viewed as vanity. Your image is important and crucial. When you look good, you feel better and can attract more people. In terms of your physical appearance, you want to look as well-groomed as possible with clean and appropriate clothing to suit the relevant occasion. This will make people respect you, as many people will judge you initially solely based on your physical appearance.

Appearance Tips

- Always dress to impress everyone who will see you on that day.
- Invest in good fragrances and perfumes.
- Make sure you look clean.
- Fake it till you make it – always appear to be confident, and don't let anyone know that you're nervous.
- Regularly maintain your hair – this will boost your self-esteem and people are impressed by a good hairstyle
- Wear the right clothes for the right occasion – you do not want to stand out for the wrong reasons. Always wear appropriate clothing depending on the occasion to make yourself and others more comfortable.

- Exercise regularly and eat healthily so that your body is in the best shape.

STEP 2: PERCEPTION

> *Life is all about perception. Positive versus negative. Whichever you choose will affect and more than likely reflect your outcomes.* - **Sonya Teclai**

There is a difference between your public image and your private image. Your public image contains your general appearance, behavior, personality traits, and your personal style. However, your private life contains your thoughts, feelings, and private fantasies.

Leaders, A-list celebrities, and politicians do their best to protect their reputations. Especially for politicians, public approval is so critical to winning votes; therefore, they must have a reputation with good qualities that people will admire and respect. People admire those to who they can relate and those whose personality traits they approve of. We can easily form an opinion and decide whether we like someone as a person based on our direct encounter with them; or what we see or hear on social media, TV, radio, or word of mouth. Machiavelli said that for a prince to maintain authority over his subjects, he must appear to have good qualities but being ready to shift and adapt when being nice is not in his best interests. In a time with so many competing rival kingdoms seeking as much power and control as possible, if a prince was too good, one of his enemies would have eventually overpowered him and taken over his kingdom. Therefore, Machiavelli instructed that a Prince should know when to be a lion, a strong force, and be aggressive against his enemies or a fox -- someone who is willing to be deceptive and cunning to manipulate his enemies when necessary. He must maintain a good image and not say anything that would make it seem as if he doesn't align with the appearance of having these good qualities. The prince also needs to be careful with his words because everyone knows what you seem, but only a few will have first-hand experience of who you really are. It's harder for people to oppose the public opinion of anyone.

Today, although you may not be a prince or a ruler, it is beneficial to appear to be a good person. If you are too nice in every encounter, people will either take advantage of your good qualities, or it may simply just not work in your favor. Ever heard of the phrase, "Nice guys finish last?" If you appear to be too bad or aggressive, people will disapprove. However, if you are willing to shift and maneuver between the lion and the fox, you can choose how to act dependent on each situation and circumstance.

On the other hand, when doing things behind closed doors, there will be times when you make mistakes and do things that you're not proud of – you are only human. But if it is in your best interests for certain things about yourself to remain private, then this needs to be contained quickly before the news spreads. Remember if you appear to have good qualities, it's harder for the few people who beg to differ to affect your reputation. However, be mindful that strong evidence and credibility can be strong enough to negatively impact your public image. Practice being the nice guy in public but yourself in private. Be wary that all actions have consequences, so be cautious of everything you do before you do something that will be hard to rectify.

CREATING YOUR OWN IMAGE

Today, it is very easy to fall into the trap where other people define our stories and future. Too many people don't have the confidence or self-esteem to truly be whatever they want to be. Sometimes it comes down to our upbringing. Within your culture, your parents may not have been willing to take many risks in the past. They may not have recognized how the world has progressively evolved from the 1970s, and 1980s to the 21st Century, and that there are now more opportunities today than there have ever been in the past.

In hip-hop culture, the expectation for a rapper is to release a few albums, maybe sign a couple of new artists under his own label imprint, like Lil Wayne did with Drake and Nicki Minaj, and then retire as a legend. But 50 Cent decided to take a better approach and shifted his image from rapper 50 Cent to business mogul Curtis Jackson. He decided to get involved in acting in his first movie *Get Rich or Die Tryin* and then acted in a few other movies afterward. He then decided to get into television and created the hit TV show *Power*. Behind the scenes, of course, some people would have been skeptical about whether *Power* would work especially because Curtis didn't have any real experience with producing a TV show prior to doing so. But Curtis realized that he had the real power of making anything he wants successful, no matter what his background or previous experience is.

You must believe in yourself, the way Curtis believed in himself. It's easy to come across a manager who is interviewing people for a job, to reject whoever he believes doesn't have the necessary experience or qualifications to be a good candidate for a job. Don't allow someone to define what you will be good at or what you are capable of. Your experience or resume doesn't define you, only you can define yourself. In general, you have the power to be who you want to be. If you want to be a doctor, actor, music artist, or open a successful business, you are the only person who can truly control if you become a success.

BE CAREFUL WHEN SUBMITTING TO AUTHORITY

Most people would view insubordination as a bad thing. Insubordination is defined as not submitting to authority. It is good to show respect to your parents, seniors, and people in positions of authority such as teachers, leaders, and law enforcement. It is usually in your best interest to show respect for their authority when you feel like it is strategically a good idea to appear submissive. This can help you avoid getting yourself into any trouble and damaging relationships. When submitting for strategic purposes, remember this is to keep up appearances. It is important to be aware that just because a figure of authority tells you something or even a professional within the field like an accountant or lawyer, it doesn't mean that they are always correct. To become a professional within a particular field, that person would need the necessary qualifications and experience within the field in order to qualify for the job. However, their experience and qualifications within the field, doesn't make them an expert or a master of every scenario or case that can occur within the field.

Let's imagine someone gets arrested; they will usually have a lawyer represent them at the police station for free, but most people believe that if you were to hire a lawyer from a firm that doesn't just represent people at the police station, they are more likely to help them win the case. What people fail to realize is the lawyer at the police station and the lawyer who works for the firm both had to complete a qualifying law degree to become a lawyer within that jurisdiction. So, why are some lawyers better than others if all lawyers typically have the same qualification? It typically comes down to the individual's style of work and the previous results from their past performance.

On a further note, there are many people currently in prison or have been released from prison who received bad advice from a lawyer. The lawyer may have advised them to plead not guilty as they have a good chance of winning the trial, but then later, the defendant was found guilty. The defendant gets sentenced to prison doing a longer sentence than he would have if he had pleaded guilty earlier and the lawyer goes home to his comfortable house.

Some people would advise a music artist to sign to a major label instead of becoming independent. A few labels may notice your buzz and send offers your way, and the music artist would be advised to accept one of these offers. The American rapper, Russ, recognized the power of not submitting to any label and went completely independent and worked hard to release his music independently via SoundCloud releasing one song per week. It wasn't until he had uploaded 98 songs that he released his first hit. After earning money from his songs and creating his very own label Diemon, he partnered up with Columbia Records, which allowed him to own 50/50 of the profits of his future music releases. Russ has been featured on the Forbes 30 under 30 lists.

Russ realized that no artist truly needs to sign to a label, and they can be successful by going independent and partnering up with a label only for distribution. Once you realize that you have the knowledge and ability to not submit, you shouldn't become arrogant or believe that you are better than others. Be humble, and when you're in a scenario where you must show respect or submit for appearances, learn how to bite your tongue unless you absolutely must speak out. You are in this for the long game and sometimes you are doing yourself a favor by being humble and submitting, not doing the other person a favor. This can help you avoid unnecessary battles and give yourself more time to plan your future.

SHIFTING PERCEPTION

As the person in control of your life, you can make a move that will make people see you in a different light. As Taylor Swift said, "We live in a world where anyone has the right to say anything about you that they want, but you have the power to prove them wrong."

Let's say you want to go to a restaurant, but it says on the website that tables are fully sold out. If you call the restaurant and say that you're an artist, you will see how the restaurant will make sure they come up with an alternative solution for you, even though all tables were previously fully booked. When you arrive on the day, they will treat you like a VIP.

Many people are afraid of public speaking. This could be fear of speaking at a conference, within a large meeting, or even just giving a speech on a special occasion. The best way to deal with the anxiety is to just deliver the presentation that you have prepared. Make sure you have practiced your presentation and feel comfortable with the material before the day you present it. When it comes to the time of delivering your presentation to your audience, always start with a strong opening to gain the interest of the audience. Now, while you are delivering your presentation, you may feel nervous and anxious during the moment, but never panic. If you make a mistake, carry on talking as if everything has gone to plan. Also, never tell your audience you are nervous about public speaking. Unless you are Beyonce who says she is nervous before delivering an incredible performance, the crowd will most likely lose respect for you if you tell them that you are nervous, and this will make matters worse. Even comedians and TV show hosts get nervous sometimes, but the tactic is to carry on.

You may have a fear of public speaking that causes you to be quieter and more reserved in social and professional meetings. If you want to appear more confident when networking,

- Always follow the 3-minute rule. Whenever you enter any room or social environment, always speak within the first three minutes. Even if it's just to greet your fellow participants or get involved with small talk. The longer you don't speak, the harder it becomes to break the ice.
- Always aim to gravitate towards the confident people and the key speakers, so you can appear as a key speaker of the meeting too. If you're shy, don't associate with other shy people, they will not help you improve your confidence skills.
- Always attend a social or networking event with the intention to meet new people and participate.
- Make a powerful entrance by greeting everyone aiming to impress them.

- If you don't feel like you will make a good effort to follow these tips, try to find a way to do so before you start going out to socialize and engage with others.

STEP 3: ALWAYS ACCOUNT FOR VARIABLE CHANGE

In life, you must always be willing to adapt and alter your strategies when appropriate. Things change over time. To maintain advantages in situations, adapting to new circumstances is essential. Pope Julius II encountered a problem. He lived in a world where if you wanted power, you needed to form alliances with other nations before making any big political moves. He wanted to take an expedition against the Italian City of Bologna, but the Venetians and the King of Spain were not in favor of this idea. However, the King of France hadn't yet negotiated with him. Any other Pope would have waited till things had resolved with the other kingdoms before making his way to Rome, but Pope Julius wasted no time. By deciding to adapt to the new circumstance and alter his strategy, he decided to march on the expedition anyway. This resulted in the Venetians fearing him, and both the King of Spain and France decided that it was better to keep him as an ally instead of a foe.

Interpretation: Princes could not solely rely on luck and fortune to lead a kingdom in a world where many other rival kingdoms are desperately attempting to seek more power. Most cautious rulers did well when luck was on their side, but when it was a time to be impetuous, they weren't willing to adapt. All the other Popes previously always ruled cautiously, unlike some of the other impetuous foreign kings and rulers.

Understand: Past actions cannot be the blueprint for all your future decisions. The world is like a forever, flowing river -- the current can change at any time. You must also be willing to change and adapt when it's needed if you want to move forward and be successful in different circumstances. Pope Julius II could have chosen the cautious route too, but caution requires patience and time, and he realized if he didn't act impetuously the other kings would have found ways to delay him. We can all change and adapt our behaviors too.

WHAT IS THE REASON FOR A CHANGE?

You need to have a reason for wanting to reinvent yourself. There may be parts of yourself that you don't like and believe need improving. You may have a certain goal that you want to reach, and you recognize that you need to make certain changes to reach that goal. The great news is that anybody can reinvent themselves; however, reinventing yourself is not easy. It requires the willingness to take good care of your appearance, be in control of how others perceive you, and become open to embracing change. When evaluating your appearance, you need to analyze which aspects of your appearance you can improve. Determine which actions you need to take to improve your appearance and make sure that they are measurable and realistic. You need to desire and be motivated for others to have a better perception of you. Therefore, it is important to observe and direct how you are perceived by others, which is why self-presentation is key. By managing your self-presentation, you can monitor how you are viewed, and supervise what other people are perceiving that benefits you. Ultimately, you are in control of whether others take you more seriously and professionally.

Regarding embracing change, you need to identify which aspects of your behavior, traits, and characteristics could be improved for you to attain better results. Do you need to change your location? Change your social circle? Do you need to improve certain habits and daily routines that will be more beneficial to your future self?

Once you identify what you want to change, set a realistic plan for how you can make these changes. Robert Downey Jr. is well known for playing Iron Man in Marvel's *Avengers*. From 1996 to 2001, he was constantly getting arrested for drug possession and lost acting roles because he couldn't make rehearsals. He also ended up spending almost a year in prison because of his drug charges. He decided he was going to make a change and after spending time in rehab, he changed his bad drug habits. He focused on working hard and becoming a reliable actor, which led to him becoming one of the biggest actors in Hollywood.

You may have heard of the famous controversial TV show *The Jerry Springer Show*. Jerry originally was a politician, and he intended for *The Jerry Springer Show* to become a political talk and debate show. After receiving poor ratings, they completely revamped the show and decided to focus on domestic issues where the guests were able to confront each other on stage. After changing the concept of the show, the ratings immediately improved, and the show ran for 27 seasons.

We all can reinvent ourselves and change our fates. If you want to dominate your destiny, you need to take control of this present moment for your future self to benefit from your actions today.

CHAPTER 7

THE POWER OF SILENCE

Silence is a true friend that never betrays. - **Confucius**

Those with the most knowledge always have the power to manipulate people who do not have enough understanding. In the early 20th Century, most of the world was colonized by European nations, which is why many countries today speak a European language. The Spanish conquered Mexico. The Portuguese Empire wanted to claim Brazil and the French controlled many states in North, Central, and West Africa.

The process of colonizing a country meant establishing foreign control over that country. Some colonizers used war and violence to take control over a country, and then stole resources from that country and enslaved many of the inhabitants. Colonization was very brutal. Countries wanted to colonize other foreign lands because they wanted ownership over the land by governing and demonstrating dominance over it.

In 1885, Leopold II, the King of Belgium, was aware of how other European nations seized power and control of other foreign lands. As the King of Belgium, he desired more power and wanted to colonize a nation of his own, the land of Congo in West Africa. He also was aware of the natural resources Congo had, such as ivory and rubber, and planned to extract them from Congo for his personal gain. His strategy was to deceive the African chiefs into peacefully transferring the legal ownership of the land directly to himself, instead of taking it by force. He succeeded with his visions by manipulating the chiefs into signing the treaty in a foreign language they did not know. By not understanding the language before they signed the treaty, it would be impossible to fully understand King Leopold's intentions and the ownership they were legally transferred to him. This led to Leopold ordering his men to steal valuable resources from Congo and slaughtering many Congolese natives. He never traveled to Congo, but he was still able to colonize and control a nation much larger than his own country.

Understand: Those with the most knowledge always have power and an advantage over those who don't have the necessary information. Acquiring as much knowledge as you can on a particular subject will always give you a greater edge. Once you have obtained it, learn to keep the knowledge more valuable by silently concealing it for yourself.

ARGUMENTS ARE A WASTE OF TIME

> *"If you argue and ranked and contradict, you may achieve a temporary victory – sometimes; but it will be an empty victory because you will never get your opponent's good will."* – **Benjamin Franklin**

As humans, we are not going to always agree with each other and sometimes people will feel very strongly about certain causes. People love others who think like them and believe in the things that they do! So, therefore, they do not like it when you disagree with them. There is an emotional attachment to most people's ideas and values. Any type of disagreement will tend to cause friction between you and the person. When two people disagree with each other in a discussion, the conversation can easily become hostile, and some people may even dislike you because you disagreed with them too strongly.

Also, it is important to remember that not everyone uses rational thinking and logic to form an opinion or an argument, which shows the type of character that they are. A lot of the views people share in an argument; show the perspective they have always used in various scenarios for a long time. Remember, most people are unlikely to change their entire way of thinking just because they have met you and have heard your strong argument.

When you are having conversations and discussions with people, and someone expresses a point that conflicts with your true way of thinking, it is better to conceal your true thoughts and let the person believe what they want to believe if it is not harmful and has no real effect on your life. If the topic is not that important, they don't need to know what you truly think. Learn how to hold back from showing whether you agree or disagree with them, to strengthen your bond and connection with them. You do not need to lie to their face and tell someone you agree if you clearly don't. It is easier than that. You can conceal your true thoughts from someone by simply not showing any type of disagreement or rebuttal to whatever they are saying. People will naturally feel and assume that you're in an agreement with them just because you haven't expressed that you disagree with them. Now, that the person feels flattered you agree with their ideas and values, they will feel more comfortable with you, and this will give you the opportunity to have a stronger influence over them.

SILENCE CREATES MYSTERY

When a person is mysterious, it is harder for others to understand you and identify one of your weaknesses. You also cause people to pay closer attention to your next moves because humans tend to feel like they have the need to figure things out that may not initially understand. When things are mysterious, people want to know more! If you are less mysterious and make moves that are easy for everyone to understand, this can lead to the downside of people seeing themselves as equal to you, or even worse, superior to you. It is not in your best interest for people to easily understand you and your motives. Increase your value and make others feel dependent on you by occasionally creating mystery behind your moves and never letting one friend or colleague completely understand you.

Never announce your moves too early! This can be a liability. When you announce your move to the world before you do it, you become more vulnerable to others trying to sabotage your goals or influence you to change your move. The best thing to do is not share every single idea that you have with your friends and family. Don't post on social media that you're planning big things next year. Not everything needs to be discussed with everyone. People are more impressed with a great product rather than a great idea. **When you're silent, there are no expectations apart from the ones you set for yourself.**

Instead of immediately announcing, do your own research if the idea is worthwhile and if you are happy with your research, then share your idea with only the people that could potentially help you.

Also, your announcements should be strong and impressive. It may appear that it came out of nowhere but, you have been silently working on it. You must also be aware that whatever you have announced needs to happen or others will hold you accountable for not following through. When rappers like Drake and Kanye West announce they are working on a new album, they are solely doing this for marketing, and they have already committed to the project. At this point, their album is coming out regardless and their announcement isn't going to negatively affect them.

On the other hand, you can't be silent and mysterious all the time. You must talk, engage, and even share things with others at some point, otherwise, it could arouse suspicion and make people skeptical of you. This will allow a person to feel more comfortable with you, but you're keeping certain things silent and you're being extremely selective with what you shared with them.

Also, working in silence and mystery works in its best form when your results are strong. When your results are strong, people will then interpret that your actions speak louder than your words.

5 WAYS TO USE THE POWER OF SILENCE

1. Make people feel like they can trust you.

One of the ways could be as simple as keeping information revealed to you, private and confidential to establish trust with people. If people feel like they can trust you, they will feel more comfortable sharing information with you. Some of the information may shock and surprise you, but ultimately you will gain more power because you have gained special private knowledge that others don't have; because you have shown that you are trustworthy. How you decide to use this information to your advantage is ultimately down to you.

2. Get straight to the point.

An effective use of exercising the power of silence is by getting straight to the point when you're speaking. When you use too many words, you risk waffling and making too many points. When people listen to someone, it's hard to remember and retain all the words the person has said. So, when you are speaking, you need to make your points very concise and direct, because the more words you say the greater likely hood of the listener forgetting some of your points.

3. Negotiating the best deals.

When you are pitching someone, you're offering or negotiating a deal. There will be a time when you will need to find out how the other person feels and establish if they are interested in your offer. Let's say you are speaking on the phone, via video conference, or in person and you decide to close your pitch by asking, "How does this sound to you?" and then remain silent. The silence in the room will automatically create discomfort for the other person, and someone will need to fill the silent void. The important thing to remember is that it should never be you who fills the silent void, especially after asking such a crucial and highly impactful question. Let the other person subconsciously feel responsible to fill the silent void by giving you a clear answer to the question you just asked them. Never ask a follow-up question or say something else before they have answered your initial high-impact question!

Whoever speaks first loses and if you let the other person speak first you will have the most leverage.

4. Let others do the talking.

It's in your best interest to create an environment and dynamic culture where other people feel comfortable speaking to you by sharing their thoughts and ideas. Some large corporations encourage innovation from their employees. Google aims to encourage innovation from its employees through different channels. They have weekly meetings where employees can ask questions and share their thoughts with senior members of the company. The trillion-dollar technology company Apple encourages innovation within its core functional organization. It has a team of Research and Development experts as well as technology experts to encourage innovation and predict how the market will respond to future products.

In other social and personal dynamics, sometimes it is better to extract information from other people and find out what their true thoughts and desires are. Sometimes it's good to ask others what they think about something. Whatever you ask, make sure you pause and do not ask a follow-up question or interrupt the person's answer. Never diminish the power of your question, always remain silent until your question is answered.

REVERSAL PERSPECTIVE

Do not overuse the power of silence or silence. If you're too silent in moments when people expect you to speak, it can arouse suspicion. People may be confused as to why you are not speaking in a scenario where it is normal to talk. However, if you say something unnecessary just because you want to avoid awkward silence, you are at risk of saying the wrong thing or something foolish that could weaken you. It is up to you to deflect suspicion by wisely using a few words to fill the void of silence. If you haven't asked a high-impact question or you're trying to extract information from the other person, then there is no need to be overly silent.

CHAPTER 8

MASTER THE ART OF INFLUENCE

> *Think twice before you speak, because your words and influence will plant the seed of either success or failure in the mind of another.* **Napoleon Hill**

We all desire to have more power in our own way. It is refreshing to have the ability to shift situations and decisions people make in our favor. When things don't go our way or someone else is trying to control a situation and steer it in a direction that you do not agree with, it can cause frustration. The world today is also very sensitive. Everything must appear to be fair or politically correct. Any discussions regarding aiming to have power, influence, and persuading others can easily be seen as being manipulative.

Throughout history, most of the leaders from Moses, Roman Emperors, and Kings were all in a strong position of power, where they were able to influence and persuade others to follow the principles they were sharing. Moses shared a positive message from God and was able to lead the Israelites out of Egypt and into the wilderness. Other leaders throughout history haven't had the most positive messages and agendas.

The popular narrative is that manipulation is very deceptive and morally corrupt. If you follow the true definition, manipulation is defined as simply having control or influence over a person or situation skillfully. Having influence and control is only bad when you are trying to deceive others who are more vulnerable than you and persuade them to do harmful things. If you don't have any control or influence over a person or situation to push your positive agenda, it will be much harder to achieve your goals. You will deal with others hoping that they are going to listen to you, as opposed to giving yourself a greater edge in order to increase your chance of people listening to you. By taking life as it comes your way and not attempting to influence situations, you will always be at the mercy of others, which can be very miserable.

On the other hand, many people are willing to deceive and manipulate you to achieve their agenda that may not be beneficial and potentially harmful to you. If you want to understand how to defend yourself against manipulative people or learn how to have influence over others, then this chapter will teach you how to increase and have greater power and influence over situations.

POWER AND INFLUENCE OVER OTHERS

It is important to understand what influence is. Influence is the ability to have an effect on the character development, the behavior of someone, or something. This means that you have the power and ability to get others to listen to you and follow your ideas.

When you have power and influence over others, you can get people to do things to help you achieve your goals. Many businesses that want to influence more people to buy their products and services will use paid advertising, such as Facebook Ads, to help them achieve their business goals for sales and growth. It also increases brand awareness and drives more traffic to their business.

Sometimes a business will pay a social media influencer to promote their product. Social media influencers have the power to digitally set trends and influence people's behavior. Kim Kardashian has successfully understood how to use influence on social media to affect consumer behavior. She has built her own brands KKW Beauty and Skims. She was able to influence other fashion markets such as Andrew Rosen and Natalie Massane to invest in her shapewear brand in 2019. As of 2021, *Forbes* reported

Kim Kardashian was now officially a billionaire with her personal equity stake in KKW Beauty and Skims exceeding the value of over $1 billion.

Many companies understand when consumers see a key figure promoting a brand, such as Kim Kardashian, who has over 200 million followers on *Instagram*, the impact her post will have on a brand or product is extremely high. If a brand uses an influencer to help promote its brand, especially an influencer that its target audience follows, this will increase the brand's chance of converting advertising into sales.

Sometimes, influence is just simply convincing another party that your idea is worth a good investment. In the early days of Facebook, Mark Zuckerberg and Sean Parker needed to influence venture capitalists and investors to invest in it. They managed to convince Peter Thiel, PayPal Co-founder, to invest in Facebook and then later in 2005, Accel Partners and Jim Breyer to invest over $12 million.

As of 2020, *Forbes* announced that the music artist Kanye West was now a billionaire. This was because of his stake in Adidas Yeezy, which had exceeded $1 billion. In 2004, Kanye West launched his debut album, which was well-received within the Hip Hop community and established him as a music artist. He had originally been working as a producer for Jay-Z, who co-owned the label Rocafella Records with Damon Dash and Kareem Burke. After spending a lot of time in the studio, he was able to influence Jay-Z, Damon Dash, and Kareem Burke to sign him under their label after demonstrating that he could rap as well as produce and convincing them he could potentially sell records. A few years later, he designed shoes for Louis Vuitton, Bape, and Giuseppe Zanotti, which did not lead to any commercial success. In 2009, he was able to negotiate a deal with Nike to release the first version of his Air Yeezy, becoming the first person who wasn't an athlete to launch a shoe deal with Nike. After Nike refused to pay Kanye royalties on Air Yeezy sales, Kanye contacted Adidas in 2013 and was able to persuade the CEO to create a new partnership to sell Air Yeezy through Adidas instead, but this time pay him his royalties.

Understand: Being persuasive is a positive thing. It can be used to convince others to make a decision that will be mutually beneficial for both you and them. Successful people can persuade and manipulate others positively by influencing people in business to purchase products, partner with them, or invest in their business. If you want to learn how to become persuasive, then you need to understand it is easier to have influence over people who know, like, and trust you. Therefore, building rapport is essential, which is a close relationship where people understand each other's ideas and communicate well. Rapport can be built very quickly even through a few minutes of talking on the phone and conveying good positive energy into the conversation. Believing in yourself is important, but it is not nice if nobody else believes in you. When people do not believe in you, they will not trust you and it will become much more difficult to persuade others and convince them of anything. Therefore, integrity is important; never give anyone a reason to feel like they cannot trust you. When you are aiming to convince people, always establish that the other person must feel like they know, like, and trust you, so that their natural guard for mistrust is lowered and they are more open and receptive to following your ideas and suggestions.

It is important to remember that history has shown us that not everybody who appears to be the leader is really in control. The Merovingian dynasty lasted from 450 to 751 AD, and it consisted of many monarchies. The Kings & Queens lived luxuriously and attended impressive ceremonies, but they had no real power or responsibilities. The true figure of power was the Mayor of the Palace who operated similarly to a Prime Minister and made important decisions. Throughout the final days of the dynasty, the power of the actual king was reduced severely. Eventually, the final Mayor of the Palace, Pepin the Short decided that since he wielded the actual power and not Childeric III who was his current king at the time;

he was going to depose Childeric III and become the king himself.

Another example of having power and influence over others was when Cardinal Richelieu became the chief minister to King Louis XIII of France in 1624. His goal was to consolidate power in France, and he was successfully able to influence King Louis to make decisions, therefore operating as the power behind the throne. In some scenarios, there is only one leader or one decision-maker that others follow. If you do not fall into this position this is still fine. Why? Because if you truly understand power, then you will know that whoever can influence the leader or decision-maker to make decisions, has power.

THE MACHIAVELLI MINDSET

You may have heard of the term Machiavellianism, which is based upon the writings and strategies of the Italian diplomat Niccolò Machiavelli. Machiavellianism is a personality style and trait which can be viewed as being manipulative and doing whatever means necessary to gain power. It encourages those who want to become future leaders or elevate to a position of authority to occasionally use deceitful or cunning techniques on others for their own personal gain.

Sometimes you will need to take advantage and use manipulation to get what you want. The world is a competitive environment, with many rival powers and potential rivals. You must do what you can to survive, succeed, and grow. In a nutshell, there are three tips that you can use from Machiavelli's writings that still apply today.

1. Destroy all rivals and potential rivals.

Cesar Borgia was an Italian cardinal who lived around the time of the 15th Century, destined for power. After his father, Pope Alexander VI, was concerned about losing to a rival power, one of his principles was to destroy any rival or potential rival to maintain power. So, he destroyed all who were of the blood of those ruling families which he had despoiled, to deprive the pope of any opportunity. He also distrusted mercenaries and auxiliaries, who were hired soldiers who fought for money, and at times, had their own personal ambitions. He was against having soldiers who weren't loyal and saw this as very dangerous. He observed that other Italian states that had mercenaries in the past always failed; and therefore, preferred to have his own troops.

Today in the 21st Century, we still have many rivals and potential rivals willing to compete with us to achieve the same goals we want. Although it is possible for multiple people to be successful, some people will be willing to take you out of your position to further their goals. In 1974, British Airways was created, and they were the leading airline company in the U.K. When Richard Branson created Virgin Atlantic in the 1980s, British Airways did not initially acknowledge them as a threat. In the 1990s, after British Airways realized and saw the strength of their new rival, they used a "Dirty Tricks" campaign against Virgin Atlantic. They committed a series of acts behind closed doors to sabotage Virgin Atlantic, and it got so bad that Richard Branson took legal action against British Airways and was awarded £3 million in compensation.

Understand: You must acknowledge all potential rivals from an early stage. If Blockbuster foresaw, they would become bankrupt in a few years and Netflix would take over, they would have worked harder to make sure they kept their competitive edge while they were the larger business over the potential future rival Netflix. You must get rid of anyone who will compete with you or has the potential to compete with you! Not all rivals and potential rivals are external. Some rivals can be friends, colleagues, and former business partners. If you have a good reason to be suspicious that someone you work with internally may become a threat in the future, then you also need to let them go!

2. Do whatever is necessary to achieve results.

In Machiavelli's writings, he suggested the end justifies the means. He believed to achieve efficient results, people will sometimes have to play dirty, and a good outcome excuses any wrongs committed to attain it. The world consists of heroes and villains but most importantly winners and losers. Winners are celebrated when they win, billionaires are celebrated when *Forbes* announces their new billionaire status. People tend to forget about all the details that the winner took on their journey in order to win, as they are too busy celebrating the winner's result. If you have kept your reputation intact and kept your dirty work private or delegated it to someone else to perform, then you can do as you please to win. There are exceptions to the rule, however, do not employ tactics that are evil and despicable! If you must play dirty, make sure it is necessary.

Chapter 4: Reading the Room, states that you must do whatever you can within your control to avoid hatred. When people hate you, then they will have a reason to turn against you. However, to be hated, there needs to be a justifiable reason for someone to hate you. As you have just learned, sometimes you may need to do things that aren't the nicest traits, such as employing dirty tactics to win. When it is time when you may need to get your hands dirty, it is better to make someone else become the face of it. This technique will help you to keep up your good appearance and you will only be associated with positive attributes.

3. Never become too nice or too generous.

Occasionally, it is very good to give back to others who are less fortunate than you. Being charitable is important, and it is good to give to others when you can do so. Machiavelli stated it is good for a prince to be seen as generous but being too generous could be dangerous. If a prince is too generous, the kingdom would be poor, and he would ultimately lose the respect of his subjects. Machiavelli encouraged it was better to give away the resources of others, rather than his own.

When large corporations donate money to charity, they appear generous. However, they are aware that the government provides them with an incentive that will help them reduce the amount of tax that they would have had to pay at the end of the financial year. The Internal Revenue Service allows U.S. corporations to receive a tax deduction if they are donating money to a qualified organization. In the U.K., a limited company will pay less corporation tax on their profits when they donate money, equipment, land, or sponsorship payments to a charity. In 2020, according to *The Chronicle of Philanthropy's* annual list of top donations, Jeff Bezos contributed a $10 billion gift. However, Amazon earned over $300 billion within the same year, and as you already know giving money to charity is a tax write-off. It is good to give, and it will benefit your public image when you do so, but remember, never become too generous.

THE 5 QUALITIES OF AN EFFECTIVE LEADER

There are people who master the art of influence well and therefore have the power to become leaders. A leader is someone who can influence and motivate others within a group or organization to follow them in order to achieve a goal. A true leader leads by example and sets the tone for the rest of the group or organization to follow. In order to become an effective leader, it is important that you possess these 5 qualities.

1. **Become a visionary.**

George Washington was the first President of the United States and one of the country's founding fathers. In 1773, a political protest known as the Boston Tea Party occurred in Massachusetts where one of the shipments belonging to the British East India Company was destroyed by the Sons of Liberty because of their opposition to the Tea Act imposed by Great Britain. Great Britain responded harshly to this in 1774 with The Intolerable Acts, which created tension between the people living within the 13 British Colonies in North America and Great Britain. Because of his previous military background, George Washington was appointed to lead the army of the 13 British Colonies in North America against Great Britain in the war for independence, also known as the American Revolution. His vision was very clear. He was determined to make sure America was an independent nation by winning the war against Great Britain. His vision became a reality, his army won the war and a few years later, the Constitution of the United States was drafted, and America was independent.

Understand: To become a leader, you need to have a clear vision. Your vision needs to be clear to you and it must be communicated to others. It was this type of thinking which enabled Washington to lead the American Revolution War which lasted over 8 years and he was still able to motivate the army to believe that they could win. When you have a clear vision, it is essential you only work with people who understand your vision and want to be a part of it. **Everyone has their own agenda and is governed by their own self-interest.** However, some people's interests can align with yours. Once a mutual interest is established, you want them to believe that working with you, will further their own interests.

Lil Wayne was a strong leader for his label Young Money Cash Money. After the success of *The Carter 3*, which sold a million copies in its first week, it became much easier for him to convince upcoming artists, that signing up with his label would be a great decision for them to make, as he understood their needs and can teach the upcoming artist to become successful just like him. This is how Lil Wayne could sign

Drake and Nicki Minaj to his label and successfully launch their careers. Both Drake and Nicki Minaj could understand Lil Wayne's vision for their careers and the label because they had seen Lil Wayne's growth as an artist and believed in his vision.

2. Know how to communicate with others.

Have you noticed that whenever you visit KFC, Pizza Hut, or Taco bell and you ask for Coke, they will always provide Pepsi and never Coca-Cola? This is because these restaurants are owned by Yum Brands Inc, which is a subsidiary of the billion-dollar multi-national beverage company, PepsiCo. Although Pepsi Co's well-known drink Pepsi-Cola is sold across the world and earns the company billions, at one point, in the early 2000s, it looked like the company was going to fail.

Indra Nooyi worked at PepsiCo in 1994 and worked her way up to CEO in 2006. She was able to solve the problems at PepsiCo by communicating her vision and coordinating plans with the rest of the shareholders. She could directly explain to them what the issues were with the company's current strategy and how they could make improvements in order to increase their market share by following her new strategic plans. Leaders must know how to skillfully speak to others and influence them to believe in their vision for achieving the shared goals of the group or organization.

A leader must know how to communicate well with others. Communication has two components: speaking and listening. As a leader, you do not need to know everything. You can learn as you go on, but you must always listen to the experts before you decide to make a big decision that you are uncertain about. John F. Kennedy was elected in 1961 as the President of the United States during the Cold War, which was a confrontation between the United States and the Soviet Union. There was a point during the war when it almost turned into a nuclear war. In 1962, the Cuban prime minister, Fidel Castro, had a secret agreement with the Soviet Union to place nuclear missiles in Cuba, which was known as the Cuban Missile Crisis.

Imagine if you were the President of the United States and you heard about this. How would you strategically respond? Would it be better to surrender or attack? The next actions John F. Kennedy took defined him as a leader who understood the importance of listening to others. He insisted he would not take any action until he heard from the National Security Council and his other key advisers. After hearing different points of view from his subordinates, he avoided making a fatal mistake by negotiating with the Soviet Union that the missiles in Cuba were dismantled and returned to the Soviet Union. Listening to others is key when you want to make good decisions.

A true leader must be empathetic and learn how to listen to others in order to understand their issues. When you focus your attention on the other person by listening to them, this will build more trust as well as strengthen your relationship with others and enable you to obtain important information that you may have missed.

3. Accept responsibility.

It can be very frustrating when somebody manages to convince you to follow one of their ideas or work with them and when it derails, they do not accept any accountability or responsibility for their faults and mistakes. These people are not leaders! A true leader accepts responsibility for a situation when expectations are not met. They can hold themselves accountable for their actions and explain to the rest of the group or organization how things can be improved moving forward. Investor and former NBA player Charles Barkley had an incident in 1991 when he spat on a fan, who allegedly made a racial slur against him. After that, he received a lot of backlash, and it negatively affected his career. Instead of whining, complaining, and protesting about how the world should have taken his side, he accepted complete responsibility for his role in the situation and he apologized to the victim and her family, then later built a friendship with them.

4. Use discernment when making decisions.

In the *Old Testament*, the Lord appeared to Solomon during the night in the form of a dream. God said, "Ask for whatever you want me to give you." Solomon asked for a discerning heart to govern his people and distinguish between right and wrong. God was pleased with Solomon for not asking for riches and wealth and promised to give him a wise and discerning heart as well as riches.

Why is a discerning heart important? Discernment is the ability to make good judgments and it is essential for all leaders. We must develop this skill over time, and it takes practice. Discernment isn't just a skill for those who want to be good leaders, every human in the world can benefit from being able to judge well to avoid making bad decisions. In relation to The Law of Cause and Effect, the cause of not being able to make a good decision will lead to the effect of negative results and the strength of the leader being questioned. If you are not yet a leader, a series of negative results will make it harder for you to influence people and ultimately affect your integrity.

Discernment can be used within business and the creative industry; discernment is essential for deciding whether something will be a good idea. In 2004, Antonio LA Reid, the CEO of Island Def Jam Music Group, at the time, offered Jay-Z the opportunity to become the President of Island Def Jam. Jay-Z's company, Rocafella Records, was already partners with Def Jam and after the previous presidents, Lyor Cohen and Kevin Liles, had moved onto Warner Music Group, this appeared to be a great opportunity for him. During the time, Jay-Z was running Def Jam, he noticed record sales were falling, and Def Jam had many executives within the company who were failing to keep the company innovative.

As the new president, Jay-Z made it his goal to revive the Def Jam label. Jay Brown worked with Jay-Z as the A&R executive for Def Jam. Most record labels have an A&R otherwise known as Artists and Repertoire, which is responsible for developing artists and finding new talent. Jay Brown received a demo tape of Rihanna, an aspiring 17-year-old singer from Barbados featuring the song *Pon De Replay*. When Jay Brown shared the demo tape with Jay-Z, he initially wasn't sure about Rihanna but invited her to the Def Jam office in New York City to audition. After she auditioned, Jay-Z took a chance with Rihanna and made sure that he could close a multi-album record deal with Rihanna that same evening. Jay-Z became very involved with the development of Rihanna as a new artist and released *Pon De Replay* as her debut single on her first album *Music in the Sun* which sold over 2 million copies worldwide.

In 2007, Jay-Z decided to leave Def Jam and started a new label called Roc Nation with Jay Brown the executive who helped discover Rihanna with him. Roc Nation signed J Cole in 2009 as its first artist and has continued to support new artists over the years. Meanwhile, due to the work Jay-Z and Jay Brown initially put in to launch Rihanna, she was able to sell a few successful album releases with Def Jam even after Jay-Z had left the label. Rihanna became a major worldwide R and B artist. She went on to create her own cosmetic brand, Fenty Beauty, and a lingerie brand that sold $100 million in revenue and in late 2021, she became a billionaire. If Jay-Z didn't have the gift of discernment and failed to act immediately, he would have missed out on the opportunity to sign Rihanna.

5. Become innovative and creative.

The Phrase "Use your imagination", is a great skill for all leaders to follow. You must be able to imagine and brainstorm which steps are necessary to take in order to achieve your goal. Reed Hasting graduated from university in the early 1990s and founded a software company called Pure Software. After a series of mergers and acquisitions that resulted in the company stock losing significant value, Reed left the company and after previously being fined $40 for returning a rented copy of Apollo 13, he decided to start a new business launching the world's first online DVD rental store. He invested money from his previous business and created a website that offered a DVD rental service that was posted through the mail. After a few years of business, he saw YouTube develop over time and in 2007 decided to change his business model to a video streaming service. After the growing popularity of the video streaming service, they decided to stop shipping DVDs. He decided to partner up with various Television Studio companies such as Paramount, MGM, Starz Play, and more to provide more films and TV shows to stream on his platform. At the time this book is written, this business has over 200 million global subscribers and is worth billions. The name of Reed Hastings' video streaming service is called Netflix Inc. Netflix has become successful because Reed Hastings has constantly been willing to innovate the business when there have been shifts in the market regarding technology and how people consume videos.

> Innovation and creativity aren't just skills for leaders, they are skills that are needed across the entire group or organization. It is your responsibility as the leader to encourage innovation and creativity. You want to make other people feel comfortable enough to suggest innovative ideas to you. This will make the group stronger overall and will be a good safeguard against future problems.

Finally, if you want to influence others to assist you with your goals or follow your vision, then you need to understand how to communicate with others, and which tactics to use in various scenarios so you can adapt to any environment. Some of the Machiavellian methods you may view as unethical and may not want to manipulate and deceive others to further your interests. Ultimately whichever leadership style and tactics you want to use in order to influence people, is totally down to you. Choose which tactics discussed in this chapter resonate with you the most, practice them and then enjoy the results.

CHAPTER 9

HOW TO DOMINATE YOUR FUTURE

You will never be greater than the thoughts that dominate your mind." **Napoleon Hill**

Do yourself a favor and make your future self proud. The problem with many people today is that they don't do themselves any favors and therefore are not happy with the results. People rarely consider the future outcomes of their decisions and the ultimate plan. Therefore, ambition is important. If you are ambitious and have goals for your future, you are a step closer to planning where you want to be in life. When you identify what your goals are, it becomes much easier to take steps toward achieving them.

Successful people set goals. You can also become a successful person. In this final chapter, you are about to learn which techniques and important rules you should follow for creating the best future version of yourself. People have literally become billionaires from knowing how to dominate their future. Once you learn these rules and apply them correctly, there is no limit to how successful you could be in the future.

1. SET BIG GOALS.

When you set a goal and you achieve it, this will give you the self-confidence to work toward achieving more big goals. The first step you need to take to dominate your future is to set big goals. Notice the word big. There is no point in setting mediocre goals you could easily achieve or have already accomplished previously. **You need to set yourself goals that are currently bigger than you.** Your big goal needs to target an accomplishment you have never reached before. Your goal needs to be very clear and intentional. Why? Well, when you set goals that are bigger than you and that you have never accomplished before, it will force and inspire you to grow. Setting mediocre goals limits you but setting larger goals will motivate you to work harder and increase your potential.

In West Philadelphia, born and raised. On the playground was where I spent most of my days. Do you recognize these words? Well, you probably heard them in the classic 90's TV show *The Fresh Prince of Bel-Air* starring Will Smith. He started off rapping in high school and was offered a scholarship to attend the Massachusetts Institute of Technology (MIT), which wanted to provide African Americans with opportunities to study. Will Smith didn't accept the scholarship because he had two big goals in mind. He wanted to become a rapper and the biggest movie star in the world.

During the 1980s, the era when Will Smith grew up, there weren't many successful rappers or movie stars from Philadelphia, let alone his local home state Pennsylvania. To set both goals was an extremely big move and required huge self-confidence. He began manifesting his goals into a reality and eventually became a local MC along with his childhood friend Jazzy Jeff. After performing and recording music over the next years, they eventually released an album together and were given the Grammy Award for Best Rap Performance. NBC then offered him the opportunity to have his own TV show called *The Fresh Prince of Bel-Air*, which launched his acting career and led to him starring in major box office movies such as *Bad Boys* and *Men in Black.* Both of his goals came true. He was a successful rapper, and he is now one of the most popular actors in the world after winning the Oscar for Best Actor for his leading role in *King Richard* -- a movie about Venus and Serena Williams being coached by their father -- during the 94th Academy Awards.

If you set goals that are above you and you are close to hitting them but slightly missed them, you will still grow because you are still aiming higher than you have ever aimed previously. Will Smith successfully reached his goals because the scope of his goals was so high that it forced him to have to work hard if he wanted to achieve his goals. He recognized there were no limitations that could stop him from reaching his goals if he had the right drive and ambition.

What are your goals? Do you have a huge goal you are trying to accomplish? Will Smith wanted to become a rapper and one of the biggest movie stars. He believed that there was nothing that could limit him from reaching his goal. He didn't feel limited because of his low social-economic background being from West Philadelphia or the color of his skin.

Now, in terms of goals, you need to figure out if there are any true limitations that could stop you from reaching your goals. If you can't think of anything that could stop you if you have the right drive, then there is no reason why you can't achieve any goal. The sky is the limit!

2. YOU MUST HAVE A STRONG PASSION FOR YOUR GOALS.

There needs to be a strong burning passion for your goals. Why did Will Smith want to be a rapper and a big movie star? Why did he set two really high goals for himself? The reason is that those were the standards he set for himself and believed he should achieve. This gave him the confidence to turn down the MIT scholarship that could have helped him become a successful engineer because he knew the scholarship would affect his ability to reach his goals. Today your goals need to be more than dreams and aspirations. They need to be a standard that you set for yourself. When a woman is dating, she knows her standards and is not willing to settle for less. You also need to know your standards when setting your big goals. You need to feel you deserve to accomplish these goals and you will not settle for less. Your goals cannot just be dreams, they must be a must!

Once you decide your goal is a must, this will influence your behavior and decisions to bring you closer to your target.

3. A GOAL WITHOUT A PLAN IS JUST A WISH.

Now that you decided what your big goals are, what is your plan for achieving these goals? When Nicki Minaj attended high school, she initially wanted to become an actress. After she graduated from a performing arts school, she struggled to take her acting career further. She also liked rap and wanted to become a rapper, which led to her signing with a local music group called Fall Force, alongside her ex-boyfriend Safaree Samuels. She eventually left the group and started independently releasing music on social media and sharing her songs with fans and potential label executives. After working hard and ensuring she was independently recording good quality songs she eventually caught the attention of Fendi. Fendi was the CEO of Dirty Money Entertainment, a local music executive from Brooklyn, New York, and after signing with him, this gave her the ability to release good quality projects from 2007 as *Playtime is Over*. She also benefited from signing with Fendi because she could be featured on a local DVD series called *The Come Up*, which is how Lil Wayne discovered her. After Lil Wayne listened to her music, he saw potential in her and signed her to his label Young Money Entertainment, which led her to become one of the world's biggest female rappers of all time. She also achieved her goal of becoming an actress by starring in movies and appearing on TV shows.

Nicki Minaj was able to achieve her goals because she had a plan. She knew she had to constantly release good music. Whether it was joining Full Force, releasing music independently on Myspace, or mixtapes when she signed to Dirty Money Entertainment, she didn't know she was going to be signed by Lil Wayne, but she knew she wanted to become a successful rapper, and by following her plan, led to Lil Wayne discovering her.

After you have an idea of what your primary goal is, you can identify other smaller supplement goals to support your main goal. After identifying your supplement goals, you want to set a deadline that can help you get further toward your main goal. For example, you could aim to earn an extra $1000 a month from your side hustle, which can help you earn enough money to invest toward taking action that can get you closer to reaching your main overall goal.

When setting your other goals, you also need a plan. The reason why you need to create a plan is that you need to set a direction to help you achieve your goals. The first step in planning toward achieving your goals is structuring your time. **You have 168 hours in a week.** If you work a 9:00 to 5:00 day job, then you have worked 40 hours in a week, and you will have 128 hours remaining. In these remaining 128 hours, you can use this time to exercise, sleep, and work on your dream. Some cases may differ including travel time to work.

4. SET YOUR DAILY TASKS.

Now that you are aware of how much spare time you have. Structure your day by organizing which tasks you need to complete on that day, what time, and how long you need to work on them. You can write your tasks within your notes or even download a task app from your smartphone. If you use *Google Tasks*, you can even set recurring tasks if you want to work at the same time every day.

You want to begin each new month with a plan, and then at the end of the month, you want to review your achievements for that month. Did you accomplish your monthly targets? Do you need to set higher goals so you could improve even further in the next few months? Always analyze your progress and find the best way to accomplish your goals.

5. NEVER TRY TO BE THE JACK OF ALL TRADES.

Have you ever heard of the phrase "Jack of all trades, master of none?" This refers to people who focus on multiple skills at the same time. Instead of mastering a specific skill, you cannot focus on too many goals at the same time, it's not productive. As mentioned above you need to have your main goal. You need to be able to dedicate enough time and focus on one goal, so you can start to master it completely before you move on.

When Apple first launched in 1976, its first goal was to create amazing personal computers. After a few years of improving the Macintosh, when Apple became profitable after a few rough years, they set their sights on a new market. They created their own portable music device called the iPod in 2001, and then the iTunes store in 2003, where people could legally download music. After the iPod became successful, a few years later they opened retail Apple stores around the world to help sell their products. But in 2007, Apple changed the game when they released the first iPhone as an attempt to enter the smartphone market, which was previously dominated by rivals such as Nokia, Motorola, Samsung, and Blackberry. A few years later, the iPhone sold billions of units and has become one of the most popular smartphones in the world today.

If Apple decided to launch the Mac, iPhone, iPad, Air pods, and all their products at the same time, it wouldn't have worked. As humans, we can only process a certain amount of information at one time. Because of the limitations of the amount of information our brain can process at the same time, we need to invest our attention more wisely. It is easier for humans to completely focus on one task as opposed to committing to multiple tasks at the same time.

Instead of multi-tasking, practice the art of single-tasking. Focus your attention on one thing at a time, until you have improved your skills to the point where you have mastered them. Once Apple focused on one product and kept developing it to make the product good, they moved on to create new products after the previous product had become successful.

If you want to dominate your future, you need to manage your desires and commit to focusing on one major goal at a time. Once you have mastered your main goal, then you can freely move on to a different goal.

6. BE RUTHLESS.

So, you have the main goal you are passionate about, and you view this goal as a standard you are going to set for yourself, you are also now aware of the supplement goals you need to accomplish to support your main goal. After establishing what your supplement goals are, you have created a weekly schedule for how you are going to work toward your main goal. Then at the end of the month, you are going to analyze your performance. But guess what, having a calendar and setting time to do work is not enough! You must be ruthless by working intensely at a high performance level. Let's say you're going to the gym, and you want to do cardio. If your plan is to do a 20-minute cardio session, but when you get to the gym, you have a 5-minute session, then you take a 5-minute break, then you run for another 5 minutes, and then you leave, you have not worked hard enough. You have not completed the 20-minute cardio run as planned; and therefore, you will not burn as many calories. How can you expect to achieve your overall goal of being healthy, if you cannot complete a basic 20-minute run that you originally planned to commit to? If you knew beforehand that you couldn't complete a 20-minute run, then that's fine if you didn't plan to do it. However, if you decide to commit to a plan because you believe you can achieve it, but then you don't commit to the plan fully, you are wasting your time and delaying your progress.

How can you work more intensely? First, you need to be focused and eliminate distractions. Do not take long breaks. Most employers who are paying you to do an 8-hour shift will not offer you a meal/lunch break longer than an hour. There are some employers who don't even offer their employees up to an hour's break. According to the U.S. Department of Labor, federal law does not require employers to pay their staff for the break and meal periods. Therefore, most employers will communicate how long the authorized break period is, with the majority offering no more than an hour for a typical day shift. If the staff member takes a longer break than authorized, federal law allows the employer to punish the employee. In the U.K., the government allows staff to have one 20-minute break if they are working over 6 hours in a day, which doesn't have to be paid.

Have you ever wondered why the law allows employers to only offer short breaks after a few hours of work? It is because they want to squeeze as much success as they can out of their employees, and they want to maintain high performance throughout the day. Breaks are designed to reduce stress with the aim to increase overall productivity. When you are working on your goals or setting time aside to work on your supplement goals, you must work at a high-performance rate and avoid taking long breaks just like you would if you were working for an employer. Keep your breaks minimal by timing them. Use them as a small rest period that will allow you to help your mind focus so you can improve your overall creativity and productivity. Remember, if you're not working intensively, then you are just wasting more of your time.

Eliminating distractions is crucial for increasing your productivity. As certain things can distract you from completing your tasks and working on your future goals. If you need to focus on work and you are being distracted by colleagues, friends, or family, find a way to work without the distraction, whether you need to change your workspace or even politely ask others if you can continue the conversation after you have finished your work!

If you're planning to work, don't spend time on social media while you're working, work intensively. If your phone distracts you, utilize airplane mode or do not disturb modes on your phone so you can focus on your work.

It is good to increase the focus of the time you are spending, so you will have enough time to work on your supplement goals. Leisure and having fun are important. Instead of constantly having leisure time outside of your day job, plan times you can use for leisure. It is important to identify which distractions in your life decrease your productivity. It could be partying, dating, drinking, or even something else. If you can identify it, then you must be relentless in eliminating distractions that will affect your ability to reach your main goal. Every time you engage in activities or make decisions that are not productive, you are creating a bad habit.

We will discuss more on habits later in this chapter, but for now, set time aside for leisure, reduce time spent on things that distract you, and eliminate any distractions that will make it harder for you to reach your main goal. It may be hard; it could be something you really love and enjoy, but remember extreme results come from extreme actions.

7. INVEST IN YOURSELF.

You need to be the best version of yourself. Poor performance doesn't lead to poor results. It leads to nothing. A good performance often leads to poor results.

You can be good at something, but not get anywhere. Why? It is because being good is not good enough?

There are many people who can cook great and delicious food. Some people decide to sell their food to make money. Most people who taste their food can agree that the food is good. Most customers will probably think that the food tastes better than McDonald's. My question is, if the food tastes better than McDonald's, then why is McDonald's the largest international restaurant and worth billions? McDonald's has strong and focused methods on ensuring that consumers believe in and love their brand. When problems occurred in the past, such as major rivalry with Burger King, and health reports that call out McDonald's for unhealthy food, they are excellent at rebuilding rapport and trust with consumers. They are always seeking new ways to become innovative such as using electronic kiosks to make it easier for customers to place their orders. They invest heavily in the right advertising using TV, billboards, and other outlets that many of their competitors also have the power to use to ensure that they are always building brand awareness. McDonald's operates restaurants in many countries, but they will still sponsor or advertise at major sporting events such as the Superbowl, Olympics, and FIFA World Cup to ensure that their brand remains strong.

Being good is not good enough, instead, you need to have an excellent performance. We have spoken about Jay-Z earlier in the book, he is a billionaire, and one of the most popular rappers of all time. Do you believe Jay-Z became who he is today because he is a good rapper? No, who cares if he is a good rapper? Jay-Z is from Brooklyn, New York, the birthplace of Hip Hop. Brooklyn has always been a competitive environment with many people today that are good at rapping. Having a good performance as a rapper was not enough, Jay-Z needed to have an excellent performance. There are many people today who are good at singing and dancing. Why do you think these people have not exceeded the accomplishments of Michael Jackson or come relatively close to his accomplishment? This is because a good singing and dancing performance is not enough! You need to have an elite singing and dancing performance. When you have a great performance, the chances of getting good results are always much higher, but when you have an elite performance, you will get the best results.

You probably have seen a singer give a good performance at a social function, but the singer isn't famous or very successful today. When Mariah Carey and Beyonce began singing, for them to become some of the biggest singers in the world, do you think they gave good performances, or do you think they gave an elite performance?

So how do you become elite? How do you give an elite performance? You need to invest in yourself by increasing your work rate and working at the best performance rate ever. If you are working out and want to increase your performance, you will increase the number of reps that you take. Increasing your reps will increase your skill level, which leads to an improvement in your results. When you start getting results, it helps you measure how good your performance was overall.

People enjoy the things that they are good at. When you start to enjoy things, you can increase your performance. This will then increase your skill level, which will lead to better results over time. If you don't increase your reps, then your skill levels won't improve. This will lead to you not getting the results you desire, which will make you enjoy the activity less. If you enjoy it less, then you will do it less, which leads to a negative cycle. If you want to earn money, you need to create value, so people are willing to pay for your product or service. The greater your results are, the greater your value is. The greater your value is, statically the more you will earn. Every decision has a cause and effect.

There are other ways you can invest in yourself. You can put money into learning new skills, such as taking education courses for something you are interested in, which you know can increase your value. You can also read books like you have done currently with this book, to improve your mindset and increase your knowledge.

There may be something that you are passionate about; let's say it's investing in property or becoming a makeup artist. Then you come across someone who is successful at what you are trying to accomplish. Then if it is possible, you may benefit by making this person your mentor. A mentor is a serious and trusted adviser. If you come across a positive role model, who's doing exactly what you want to do, y having them onboard as a mentor, you could learn so much valuable knowledge about how to achieve the results that you desire. Even Machiavelli said, *"For since men for the most part follow,"* meaning that you should know that you cannot entirely imitate a great person, but you should always try. Why did he advise this? He knew there was a benefit to learning from those who had been successful in history. By creating the opportunity to be mentored and being closer to the powerful role model you admire, it can give you a greater advantage. Having a mentor is like a special cheat code and a shortcut to success within that field. This mentor has made many mistakes, so they can teach you how to avoid them and they can overall help you get to your goal faster. To become elite, you must keep investing in yourself and learning.

8. DECISIONS LEAD TO HABITS.

Every decision you make trains you toward making a subconscious habit. The more you decide to plan to do something unproductive, the more likely you are to do it. Consider the long-term effect of every decision you make to analyze which decisions are beneficial, and which are not. Are the habits you developed from the long-term effect of your past decisions helping you get closer to your goals, or do they deter you?

You need to identify your bad habits and then remove them. When you identify your bad habits, you realize the reason you do these habits is that you want instant gratification or benefit from that habit. People eat fast food because they know they will get instant gratification from eating a meal that tastes nice. People will decide not to save money and will spend recklessly because they want that instant gratification in buying things they enjoy. When you enjoy things, this is known as pleasure. Your body creates a neuromodulatory molecule called dopamine, which allows you to feel pleasure, satisfaction, and motivation. People continue to practice bad habits because they are focused on seeking dopamine.

You need to rewire your thinking and behavior. A good way to start is to start a dopamine detox. During a dopamine detox, you will need to avoid anything that sets off dopamine triggers for a set period. This means eliminating habits you are aware of that are bad, which give you pleasure such as avoiding social media, junk food, video games, drugs, or any other habit that doesn't benefit you long term. **Your aim is to change your mindset from seeking instant gratification to delayed gratification.** Delayed gratification is when you resist immediately available rewards hoping to obtain a more-valued reward in the future. If you want to make your future self proud, then you need to practice smart decisions today that will benefit you in the future. If you know certain decisions that require you to exercise more discipline and self-control at first, will lead to a greater result in the future. You need to practice delayed gratification. For example, resisting the temptation to buy junk food when you know that you're on a diet has benefits. This will build your discipline and delay your gratification. You may be on a diet, and you know that if you stick to it, you will achieve your overall goal of having a healthy body. With delayed gratification, you resist that gratification of junk food to obtain a more-valued reward in the future.

Understand: Without discipline, you will always live a reckless life. Not only do you need to work on your physical health at the gym, but you also need to work and train your mindset. If you are not willing to make small sacrifices for your goals, then your goals will be sacrificed! You can choose to either sacrifice your instant gratification or sacrifice your future goals. Either way, something is going to be sacrificed so you might as well make the right choice.

Let's say you love ordering junk food to your house. By doing this you know you're sacrificing your body because this food isn't healthy for you. You are also sacrificing your money because ordering food is usually more expensive than cooking. The additional expenses from ordering junk food will make it harder for you to save money every month.

The decisions and actions you make today will affect your future. Hopefully, after reading this book, you have learned new strategies and techniques to help you make good decisions in the present to benefit yourself in the future. As the wise man, Mahatma Gandhi once said, "The future depends on what you do today."

REMEMBER:

MAKE YOUR FUTURE SELF RICH

Many people want to become millionaires and financially free, but they don't know how to even make six figures, until now! Financial literacy and education are key for you to achieve your financial goals. Remember how entrepreneurs think and behave financially. Keep practicing the skills you have learned and the mindset that you need to apply in order to achieve your financial goals.

STRATEGIC THINKING

You must be clever when dealing with people. The decisions and actions you take, especially when dealing with people, will have a positive or negative result in the future.

You owe it to yourself to be ten steps ahead of everyone and see how a move will play out before deciding which decisions and actions will be the most beneficial to you.

OPPORTUNITIES COME TO THOSE WHO CREATE THEM

Life is full of opportunities. Many people would be more successful than they are today if they took more opportunities that came their way. A major problem is that not everyone will take risks. By being unwilling to take risks, they will waste the opportunity.

Remember what you have learned in this chapter about how to spot opportunities, the importance of taking risks, and how to become a high achiever. Ultimately, it is up to you whether you want to take the next opportunity in front of you or lose the chance.

READING THE ROOM

We all desire power and for things to benefit us. The ability to understand how people around you think is vital for knowing how to influence them to do the things that you want. By understanding how using emotional intelligence can be applied as a powerful tool, you can interpret people's thoughts much easier and learn how to predict their next moves.

By reading the room and knowing in advance what your opponent's next move will be, the power and leverage are in your hands to benefit from.

AVOID THE JOKER OR BECOME PART OF THE CIRCUS

Having the wrong people around you has caused others to lose empires, million-dollar businesses, and many other things. By associating yourself with the wrong people, their misfortunate and bad traits can have a dangerous effect on your ventures. The longer they are around, the greater harm they can cause, and you will ultimately be the person suffering the consequences of their actions. In a world filled with winners and losers, heroes, and villains, you must avoid the losers and the villains at all costs, or your story will end up like theirs. Remember, you become like the people you are around.

REINVENT YOURSELF

You are the master of your appearance and how other people perceive you. You have the power to change things and make improvements that will ultimately create more power and respect for your future self. The person who will not accept things and not make improvements is doomed.

If you want others to view you better, then practice using the cheat codes you have learned in this chapter to adapt their appearance and change the way others perceive you.

THE POWER OF SILENCE

The greatest moves are made in silence. Not everybody needs to know your next move until you want to reveal it. At times, when we are not silent, we can also reveal too much which can create liabilities. Your silence instead will make you appear more mysterious to others, and it will be harder for people to discover things about you that you don't want them to know. Do not allow emotions to distract you from your goals, remain calculated and silent if you want to accomplish great things.

MASTER THE ART OF INFLUENCE

The elite and most powerful people understand the importance of having control and influence over the market to achieve their goals. It is always preferable for you to understand how to use influence and persuasion to further your own agendas in social and business relationships.

Learning how to influence doesn't mean that you need to be manipulative, instead, this chapter will teach you how to impact the behaviors, choices, and opinions of others to accomplish a result that's mutually beneficial for both of you.

HOW TO DOMINATE YOUR FUTURE

If you want to accomplish greater things in life, then you need to have greater goals. When you commit to a greater goal and decide to proactively act on it, you will perform inevitably greater which will yield greater results. This chapter will teach you how to eliminate distractions, focus on mastering your craft, and outperform others within your field so that you can create the best future version of yourself.

If you want to start working on your future, start now.

ABOUT THE AUTHOR

Shaquille Moore is an author, entrepreneur, and creative from South London. Shortly after graduating from a university with a law degree, he discovered his passion for business and entrepreneurship. After learning lessons from his previous life experiences, he is passionate about motivating others to achieve their goals and to create the best future version of themselves.

Printed in Great Britain
by Amazon